THE ENCYCLOPEDIA OF PSYCHOACTIVE DRUGS

SERIES 1

The Addictive Personality
Alcohol and Alcoholism
Alcohol Customs and Rituals
Alcohol Teenage Drinking
Amphetamines Danger in the Fast Lane
Barbiturates Sleeping Potion or Intoxicant?
Caffeine The Most Popular Stimulant
Cocaine A New Epidemic
Escape from Anxiety and Stress
Flowering Plants Magic in Bloom
Getting Help Treatments for Drug Abuse
Heroin The Street Narcotic
Inhalants The Toxic Fumes

LSD Visions or Nightmares?
Marijuana Its Effects on Mind & Body
Methadone Treatment for Addiction
Mushrooms Psychedelic Fungi
Nicotine An Old-Fashioned Addiction
Over-The-Counter Drugs Harmless or Hazardous?
PCP The Dangerous Angel
Prescription Narcotics The Addictive Painkillers
Quaaludes The Quest for Oblivion
Teenage Depression and Drugs
Treating Mental Illness
Valium and Other Tranquilizers

SERIES 2

Bad Trips
Brain Function
Case Histories
Celebrity Drug Use
Designer Drugs
The Downside of Drugs
Drinking, Driving, and Drugs
Drugs and Civilization
Drugs and Crime
Drugs and Diet
Drugs and Disease
Drugs and Emotion
Drugs and Pain
Drugs and Perception
Drugs and Pregnancy
Drugs and Sexual Behavior

Drugs and Sleep
Drugs and Sports
Drugs and the Arts
Drugs and the Brain
Drugs and the Family
Drugs and the Law
Drugs and Women
Drugs of the Future
Drugs Through the Ages
Drug Use Around the World
Legalization: A Debate
Mental Disturbances
Nutrition and the Brain
The Origins and Sources of Drugs
Substance Abuse: Prevention and Treatment
Who Uses Drugs?

DRUGS
&
SLEEP

GENERAL EDITOR
Professor Solomon H. Snyder, M.D.

*Distinguished Service Professor of
Neuroscience, Pharmacology, and Psychiatry at
The Johns Hopkins University School of Medicine*

•

ASSOCIATE EDITOR
Professor Barry L. Jacobs, Ph.D.

*Program in Neuroscience, Department of Psychology,
Princeton University*

•

SENIOR EDITORIAL CONSULTANT
Joann Rodgers

*Deputy Director, Office of Public Affairs at
The Johns Hopkins Medical Institutions*

THE ENCYCLOPEDIA OF PSYCHOACTIVE DRUGS

SERIES 2

DRUGS

& SLEEP

LYNNE LAMBERG

CHELSEA HOUSE PUBLISHERS

NEW YORK • PHILADELPHIA

EDITOR-IN-CHIEF: Nancy Toff
EXECUTIVE EDITOR: Remmel T. Nunn
MANAGING EDITOR: Karyn Gullen Browne
COPY CHIEF: Juliann Barbato
PICTURE EDITOR: Adrian G. Allen
ART DIRECTOR: Giannella Garrett
MANUFACTURING MANAGER: Gerald Levine

Staff for DRUGS AND SLEEP:

SENIOR EDITOR: Jane Larkin Crain
ASSOCIATE EDITOR: Paula Edelson
ASSISTANT EDITOR: Michele A. Merens
EDITORIAL ASSISTANT: Laura-Ann Dolce
COPY EDITOR: Michael Goodman
ASSOCIATE PICTURE EDITOR: Juliette Dickstein
PICTURE RESEARCHER: Matthew Miller
DESIGNER: Victoria Tomaselli
DESIGN ASSISTANT: Donna Sinisgalli
COVER ILLUSTRATION: *The Sleeping Gypsy* by Henri Rousseau, courtesy of The Museum of Modern Art.

CREATIVE DIRECTOR: Harold Steinberg

3 5 7 9 8 6 4

Library of Congress Cataloging-in-Publication Data

Lamberg, Lynne.
  Drugs and sleep.
  (The Encyclopedia of psychoactive drugs. Series 2)
  Bibliography: p.
  Includes index.
  1. Sleep disorders—Treatment—Juvenile literature. 2. Sleep—Physiological aspects—Juvenile literature. 3. Hypnotics—Juvenile literature. [1. Sleep. 2. Drugs]
I. Title. II. Series.
RC547.L35 1988   616.8'49   87-14582

ISBN 1-55546-213-8
     0-7910-0793-6 (pbk.)

CONTENTS

Sleep presumably serves a vital purpose, though scientists have yet to define it precisely. Like his peers, this napping infant probably averages about 12 hours of sleep each day, including a midday nap.

FOREWORD

In the Mainstream
of American Life

One of the legacies of the social upheaval of the 1960s is that psychoactive drugs have become part of the mainstream of American life. Schools, homes, and communities cannot be "drug proofed." There is a demand for drugs — and the supply is plentiful. Social norms have changed and drugs are not only available—they are everywhere.

But where efforts to curtail the supply of drugs and outlaw their use have had tragically limited effects on demand, it may be that education has begun to stem the rising tide of drug abuse among young people and adults alike.

Over the past 25 years, as drugs have become an increasingly routine facet of contemporary life, a great many teenagers have adopted the notion that drug taking was somehow a right or a privilege or a necessity. They have done so, however, without understanding the consequences of drug use during the crucial years of adolescence.

The teenage years are few in the total life cycle, but critical in the maturation process. During these years adolescents face the difficult tasks of discovering their identity, clarifying their sexual roles, asserting their independence, learning to cope with authority, and searching for goals that will give their lives meaning.

Drugs rob adolescents of precious time, stamina, and health. They interrupt critical learning processes, sometimes forever. Teenagers who use drugs are likely to withdraw increasingly into themselves, to "cop out" at just the time when they most need to reach out and experience the world.

A wealthy Roman suffers the agonies of insomnia. Through the ages, people with sleep disorders have resorted to numerous potions and strategies in search of that much-needed "good night's rest."

Fortunately, as a recent Gallup poll shows, young people are beginning to realize this, too. They themselves label drugs their most important problem. In the last few years, moreover, the climate of tolerance and ignorance surrounding drugs has been changing.

Adolescents as well as adults are becoming aware of mounting evidence that every race, ethnic group, and class is vulnerable to drug dependency.

Recent publicity about the cost and failure of drug rehabilitation efforts; dangerous drug use among pilots, air traffic controllers, star athletes, and Hollywood celebrities; and drug-related accidents, suicides, and violent crime have focused the public's attention on the need to wage an all-out war on drug abuse before it seriously undermines the fabric of society itself.

The anti-drug message is getting stronger and there is evidence that the message is beginning to get through to adults and teenagers alike.

The Encyclopedia of Psychoactive Drugs hopes to play a part in the national campaign now underway to educate young people about drugs. Series 1 provides clear and comprehensive discussions of common psychoactive substances, outlines their psychological and physiological effects on the mind and body, explains how they "hook" the user, and separates fact from myth in the complex issue of drug abuse.

Whereas Series 1 focuses on specific drugs, such as nicotine or cocaine, Series 2 confronts a broad range of both social and physiological phenomena. Each volume addresses the ramifications of drug use and abuse on some aspect of human experience: social, familial, cultural, historical, and physical. Separate volumes explore questions about the effects of drugs on brain chemistry and unborn children; the use and abuse of painkillers; the relationship between drugs and sexual behavior, sports, and the arts; drugs and disease; the role of drugs in history; and the sophisticated drugs now being developed in the laboratory that will profoundly change the future.

Each book in the series is fully illustrated and is tailored to the needs and interests of young readers. The more adolescents know about drugs and their role in society, the less likely they are to misuse them.

Joann Rodgers
Senior Editorial Consultant

An illustration from a 19th-century edition of Sleeping Beauty. *Sleep has long been regarded as a mysterious entity, and many tales and legends endow it with magical properties.*

INTRODUCTION

The Gift of Wizardry
Use and Abuse

JACK H. MENDELSON, M.D.
NANCY K. MELLO, Ph.D.
Alcohol and Drug Abuse Research Center
Harvard Medical School—McLean Hospital

Dorothy to the Wizard:

"I think you are a very bad man," said Dorothy.
"Oh no, my dear; I'm really a very good man; but I'm a very bad Wizard."
—from THE WIZARD OF OZ

Man is endowed with the gift of wizardry, a talent for discovery and invention. The discovery and invention of substances that change the way we feel and behave are among man's special accomplishments, and, like so many other products of our wizardry, these substances have the capacity to harm as well as to help. Psychoactive drugs can cause profound changes in the chemistry of the brain and other vital organs, and although their legitimate use can relieve pain and cure disease, their abuse leads in a tragic number of cases to destruction.

Consider alcohol — available to all and yet regarded with intense ambivalence from biblical times to the present day. The use of alcoholic beverages dates back to our earliest ancestors. Alcohol use and misuse became associated with the worship of gods and demons. One of the most powerful Greek gods was Dionysus, lord of fruitfulness and god of wine. The Romans adopted Dionysus but changed his name to Bacchus. Festivals and holidays associated with Bacchus celebrated the harvest and the origins of life. Time has blurred the images of the Bacchanalian festival, but the theme of drunkenness as a major part of celebration has survived the pagan gods and remains a familiar part of modern society. The term "Bacchanalian Festival" conveys a more appealing image than "drunken orgy" or "pot party," but whatever the label, drinking alcohol is a form of drug use that results in addiction for millions.

The fact that many millions of other people can use alcohol in moderation does not mitigate the toll this drug takes on society as a whole. According to reliable estimates, one out of every ten Americans develops a serious alcohol-related problem sometime in his or her lifetime. In addition, automobile accidents caused by drunken drivers claim the lives of tens of thousands every year. Many of the victims are gifted young people, just starting out in adult life. Hospital emergency rooms abound with patients seeking help for al-cohol-related injuries.

Who is to blame? Can we blame the many manufacturers who produce such an amazing variety of alcoholic beverages? Should we blame the educators who fail to explain the perils of intoxication, or so exaggerate the dangers of drinking that no one could possibly believe them? Are friends to blame — those peers who urge others to "drink more and faster," or the macho types who stress the importance of being able to "hold your liquor"? Casting blame, however, is hardly con-structive, and pointing the finger is a fruitless way to deal with the problem. Alcoholism and drug abuse have few cul-prits but many victims. Accountability begins with each of us, every time we choose to use or misuse an intoxicating substance.

It is ironic that some of man's earliest medicines, derived from natural plant products, are used today to poison and to intoxicate. Relief from pain and suffering is one of society's many continuing goals. Over 3,000 years ago, the Therapeutic Papyrus of Thebes, one of our earliest written records, gave instructions for the use of opium in the treatment of pain. Opium, in the form of its major derivative, morphine, and similar compounds, such as heroin, have also been used by many to induce changes in mood and feeling. Another ex-ample of man's misuse of a natural substance is the coca leaf, which for centuries was used by the Indians of Peru to reduce fatigue and hunger. Its modern derivative, cocaine, has im-portant medical use as a local anesthetic. Unfortunately, its increasing abuse in the 1980s clearly has reached epidemic proportions.

The purpose of this series is to explore in depth the psychological and behavioral effects that psychoactive drugs have on the individual, and also, to investigate the ways in which drug use influences the legal, economic, cultural, and even moral aspects of societies. The information presented here (and in other books in this series) is based on many clinical and laboratory studies and other observations by people from diverse walks of life.

Over the centuries, novelists, poets, and dramatists have provided us with many insights into the sometimes seductive but ultimately problematic aspects of alcohol and drug use. Physicians, lawyers, biologists, psychologists, and social scientists have contributed to a better understanding of the causes and consequences of using these substances. The authors in this series have attempted to gather and condense all the latest information about drug use and abuse. They have also described the sometimes wide gaps in our knowledge and have suggested some new ways to answer many difficult questions.

One such question, for example, is how do alcohol and drug problems get started? And what is the best way to treat them when they do? Not too many years ago, alcoholics and drug abusers were regarded as evil, immoral, or both. It is now recognized that these persons suffer from very complicated diseases involving deep psychological and social problems. To understand how the disease begins and progresses, it is necessary to understand the nature of the substance, the behavior of addicts, and the characteristics of the society or culture in which they live.

Although many of the social environments we live in are very similar, some of the most subtle differences can strongly influence our thinking and behavior. Where we live, go to school and work, whom we discuss things with — all influence our opinions about drug use and misuse. Yet we also share certain commonly accepted beliefs that outweigh any differences in our attitudes. The authors in this series have tried to identify and discuss the central, most crucial issues concerning drug use and misuse.

Despite the increasing sophistication of the chemical substances we create in the laboratory, we have a long way to go in our efforts to make these powerful drugs work for us rather than against us.

The volumes in this series address a wide range of timely questions. What influence has drug use had on the arts? Why do so many of today's celebrities and star athletes use drugs, and what is being done to solve this problem? What is the relationship between drugs and crime? What is the physiological basis for the power drugs can hold over us? These are but a few of the issues explored in this far-ranging series.

Educating people about the dangers of drugs can go a long way towards minimizing the desperate consequences of substance abuse for individuals and society as a whole. Luckily, human beings have the resources to solve even the most serious problems that beset them, once they make the commitment to do so. As one keen and sensitive observer, Dr. Lewis Thomas, has said,

> There is nothing at all absurd about the human condition. We matter. It seems to me a good guess, hazarded by a good many people who have thought about it, that we may be engaged in the formation of something like a mind for the life of this planet. If this is so, we are still at the most primitive stage, still fumbling with language and thinking, but infinitely capacitated for the future. Looked at this way, it is remarkable that we've come as far as we have in so short a period, really no time at all as geologists measure time. We are the newest, youngest, and the brightest thing around.

DRUGS
&
SLEEP

Washington Irving's legendary character Rip Van Winkle awakens from his 20-year slumber. Actually, most people spend the equivalent of 20 to 25 years asleep during their lifetime.

AUTHOR'S PREFACE

Rip Van Winkle, according to the famous tale authored by the 19th-century American writer Washington Irving, slept for 20 years. Rip's feat is unique in that he slept straight through; most people normally spend 20 to 25 years of their lives asleep.

Sleep presumably serves a vital purpose. Why else would animals put themselves at risk of attack by predators for sustained periods? For humans, sleep seems to be necessary for rest and restoration of both body and mind and may aid learning and memory.

Unfortunately, sleep is not always easily obtained in the amount or quality desired. One out of three American adults reports occasional or frequent trouble in falling asleep, that is, insomnia. Difficulty in sleeping is a key symptom of jet lag and a common complaint of rotating shift workers, who now constitute one in four American workers.

The desire for a good night's sleep prompts millions of people to use a variety of sleep aids, including drugs known as hypnotics, that are designed to induce and sustain sleep. Indeed, drugs are prescribed and used for sleep problems more often than for any other therapeutic purpose.

This book explores the nature of sleep and of insomnia, the effects — both good and bad — of hypnotic drugs on sleep and waking behavior, and ways to combat insomnia without the use of drugs.

An artist's rendering of prehistoric man. The earliest cave dwellers established the concept of home as a place to sleep.

CHAPTER 1

THE NATURE OF SLEEP

The need to sleep is an organizing force for living creatures. Rabbits retreat to holes, bears to caves, birds to nests. The earliest humans were wanderers who carried with them animal hides on which they slept. The first cave dwellers established the concept of home as a place to sleep. Today, most real estate advertisements define the size of an apartment or house by its number of bedrooms.

Sleep has long been regarded with awe and mystery and considered a time of both peace and danger. According to ancient Greek mythology, the goddess of night, Nyx, had twin sons: Hypnos, the god of sleep, and his brother, Thanatos, the god of death. Primitive peoples thought the soul left the body during sleep. They were careful not to awaken a sleeper, because the soul might be away and not have time to get back. They believed that someone awakened without his soul might become ill or even die. The fear of dying while asleep is reflected in a still common bedtime prayer: "Now I lay me down to sleep, I pray the Lord my soul to keep. If I should die before I wake, I pray the Lord my soul to take."

A normal night's sleep is not as deep as the winter hibernation of animals and is not truly a state of unconsciousness. People who are asleep can hear such noises as passing traffic, falling rain, or a baby's cry. They can feel a draft of

A detail from Raphael's School of Athens *depicts Plato (left) and Aristotle deep in conversation. Plato wrote, "Even in good men there is a lawless wild-beast nature, which peers out in sleep."*

cold air or the warmth of too many blankets. They can smell smoke. And their minds do not stop functioning — their thinking takes the form of dreams.

Many cultures believed dreams show the places visited, people encountered, and other adventures of the sleeper's wandering soul. Dreams also have been regarded as messages from another world or a part of the self that is not usually accessible during waking hours. The ancient Egyptians sought religious inspiration for dreams that would illuminate their waking lives. Plato wrote in the fourth century B.C.E. (B.C.E. means Before the Common Era, the same period as B.C.), "Even in good men there is a lawless wild-beast nature, which peers out in sleep," a concept elaborated at the beginning of this century by the father of psychoanalysis, Sigmund Freud. Freud saw dreams as the "royal road" to the unconscious. Dakota Indians of the American plains hung dream nets over their sleeping babies; they hoped that frightening dreams would be caught and held firmly by the net, whereas pleasant dreams would slip through a small hole in its center to reach the child.

Until this century, scientists regarded sleep as a unitary and passive state. But the development of the electroencephalograph (EEG) in the 1920s made it possible to measure the natural electrical activity of the brain through electrodes attached to the forehead and scalp and connected by wires to a recording device. Recordings made in the 1930s first identified cycles of specific brain wave patterns during sleep, but researchers could only guess at the significance of these cycles.

REM and NREM Sleep

In 1952, Nathaniel Kleitman and Eugene Aserinsky of the University of Chicago decided to examine the activity of not only the brain during sleep, but also that of eye muscles, in order to see if the slow, rolling movements that occur as people fall asleep also take place during sleep. They discovered that periodically, eyes move rapidly during sleep, much as they do when people are awake. When sleepers were awakened during what came to be called Rapid Eye Movement

Sigmund Freud, the father of psychoanalysis, saw dreams as the "royal road" to the unconscious.

(REM) periods and were asked what was going through their minds, the great majority typically described vivid, storylike dreams with extensive visual imagery. When awakened during non-REM, or NREM, periods, most reported no dreams or simply mundane thoughts, much like those of everyday waking life.

Brain activity during NREM periods is slow and uniform. In REM sleep, by contrast, brain activity is irregular and resembles that which takes place during time spent awake. Hence REM sleep was termed "active sleep" and NREM sleep, "quiet sleep." Studies of hundreds of sleepers of all ages showed that normal sleep follows a predictable pattern: Periods of quiet and active sleep alternate in cycles that last approximately 90 minutes.

The two sleeping states show curious paradoxes. During REM sleep, muscles that move the arms, legs, and rest of the body are paralyzed; people thus are prevented from jumping out of bed and acting out their dreams. By contrast, during NREM sleep, the body moves frequently; indeed, people shift positions dozens of times a night in this type of sleep, which is probably part of the body's system for self-protection. Such movement prevents pressure sores, exercises muscles, and keeps joints flexible. Blood pressure is low, and heart rate and breathing are slow and steady in NREM sleep, more variable in REM sleep.

After "lights out" on a typical night, most young adults fall asleep within seven minutes. Their sleep starts with NREM sleep, which is divided into three (originally, four) stages, identified as stages 1, 2, and 3-4, representing the progression from the lightest to the deepest sleep. The distinction between stages is based on how loud a noise it takes to trigger awakening and on the characteristic brain waves that occur in each stage.

In stage 1, thoughts drift. Many people report feeling that they are floating or falling. Indeed, they sometimes experience a sudden jerk of the leg, arm, or whole body. They may have brief, dreamlike reveries. Heart rate, blood pressure, and temperature start to fall. On the brain wave recording, alpha waves, which characterize relaxed wakefulness and cycle 8 to 13 times per second, gradually give way to theta waves, which cycle 4 to 8 times per second.

Characteristic brief bursts of brain activity, apparent to the eye of a trained reader of the EEG record, serve as markers

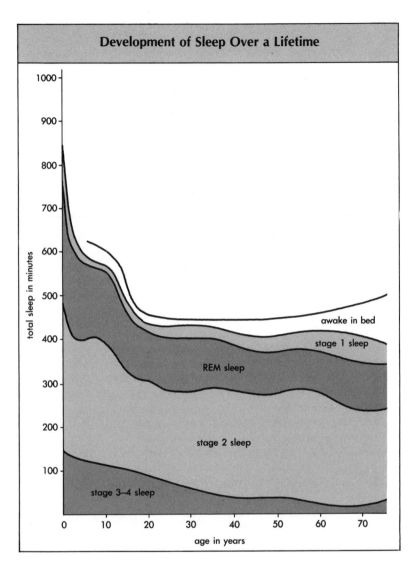

Development of Sleep Over a Lifetime

total sleep in minutes (y-axis)

age in years (x-axis)

awake in bed

stage 1 sleep

REM sleep

stage 2 sleep

stage 3–4 sleep

that the sleeper has moved into stage 2 sleep. If awakened at this time, some people report short thoughts, whereas others deny they were asleep. A few report vivid dreams.

Between 15 and 30 minutes after falling asleep, people enter stage 3-4. The brain waves characteristic of this stage, known as delta waves, are the largest and slowest of all, cycling fewer than four times per second. Originally, scientists attempted to distinguish between stages 3 and 4 by the frequency of the delta waves, but today most scientists combine these stages. If awakened at this time, people generally recognize that they were sleeping; indeed, sometimes they are so deeply asleep that they regain alertness only after a few

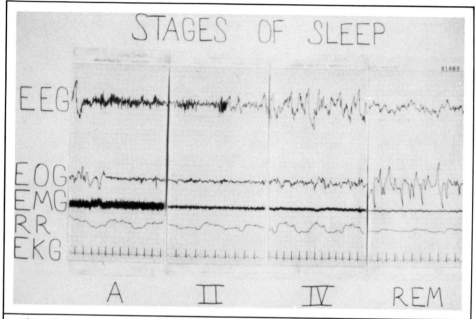

This chart is a record of the changes in electrical brain activity, eye movement, muscle tone, respiration rate, and heart rate during some of the different stages of sleep.

minutes and recall thoughts poorly. Heart rate, blood pressure, and temperature are lower and more even. Sleep in stage 3-4 lasts about an hour in a young adult; the sleeper then returns to stage 2 and quickly enters REM sleep.

The first period of REM sleep occurs about 70 to 90 minutes after sleep begins and lasts roughly 10 to 15 minutes, often serving as a "preview" for the "coming attractions" of dreams occurring later in the night. The heart rate goes up, blood pressure and other metabolic rates increase, and body temperature becomes more uneven. Brain waves are irregular and small and show bursts of a "sawtooth" pattern, so named for its physical resemblance to a saw blade. Soon the sleeper returns to NREM sleep, and the cycle repeats.

As sleep continues, NREM periods become shorter and lighter, and REM periods, longer. One consequence is that the longer sleep continues, the longer dreams become. When people awaken spontaneously in the morning, that is, without an alarm clock or a knock on the door, they usually awaken from or shortly after a REM period, making the last dream of the night the easiest to remember.

Young adults spend about 5% of their total sleep time in stage 1, 50% in stage 2, 20 to 25% in stage 3-4, and 20 to 25% in REM sleep.

Animals get varying amounts of sleep each day, from as few as 2 or 3 hours for horses and cows, to as many as 20 hours for the giant sloth. Younger animals typically sleep more than older ones, and that is true for humans as well.

Newborns may sleep 16 to 18 hours a day, and they spend half of their sleep time in REM sleep. The proportion of time spent in REM sleep drops to about one third of sleep time by age 2, and to about one fifth by age 10. It stays at that level until extreme old age. The need for large amounts of REM sleep in early life has led researchers to suggest that REM sleep is crucial for learning and memory.

In their natural habitat, some species of bear spend the coldest part of the year in hibernation, or deep sleep, in sheltered dens.

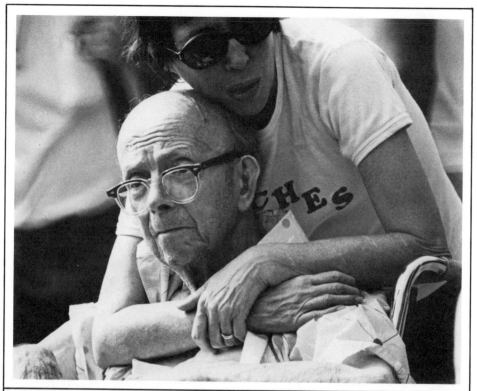

As people age, they spend less time in deep sleep. Restless sleep is one of the most common complaints of the elderly.

Between young adulthood and old age, the proportion of the deep sleep of stage 3-4 falls from about 20 to 25% of sleep time to virtually 0%, whereas the proportion of the light sleep of stage 2 increases from about 50 to 70% and is accompanied by an increase in time spent awake during the night. Light or restless sleep, a common complaint of the elderly, is reflected by changes in the EEG record as people grow older.

Newborns typically wake and sleep six to eight times throughout the day, but by three months of age, they have learned to get most of their sleep at night. (If their parents worked at night and slept during the day seven days a week, their babies would learn to sleep during the day.) The typical 2-year-old child sleeps about 12 hours a day, including a short midday nap. By the age of 4, most children abandon napping and sleep about 10 hours straight. From about age 6 until about age 13, children get about 9 hours of sleep, and they are fully alert all day long.

Teenagers regard being able to control the amount of sleep they get and the time it is taken as a privilege of adulthood. When Stanford University researchers asked 11th and 12th graders, "Do you enjoy staying up late?" two thirds answered "Yes."

Most teens — like most adults — shortchange themselves on sleep during the week and sleep longer on weekends. Sleeping late on Saturdays and Sundays thus reflects a genuine need for more sleep, rather than, as parents often complain, "sheer laziness." But late hours and insufficient sleep do not fully account for daytime sleepiness in adolescents. Rather, it appears to be an inborn trait.

Napping

Recent research suggests that humans have a tendency to desire 2 sleep periods every 24 hours, one lasting roughly 8 hours overnight and the other lasting about an hour in the middle of the day. The majority of the world's population satisfies the second need by taking a midday nap. It is only in those Western societies, such as the United States, that adhere to a nine-to-five schedule, that midday naps by adults generally are out of favor.

There are, however, certain segments of American society that enjoy the practice of taking afternoon naps. These groups include not only the very young and the very old, but also college students. Because these students generally have classes only a few hours a day and can structure their day as they wish, their behavior may reflect what most people would do if given the same opportunity. University of Pennsylvania researchers report that half of all college students nap one or more times a week. Three out of four say that they nap to make up for lost sleep, and they average one to two naps a week. The others, who say they simply enjoy napping, nap three to five times a week.

The elderly nap because they are less able to sustain sleep at night. It is a myth, sleep researchers say, that people need less sleep as they grow older, although the amount they get is often less than they desire. Although sleep becomes more fragile with age, poor sleep is not an inevitable part of aging. The elderly are, however, more likely to complain of insomnia and to use sleeping pills more often than younger adults.

For troubled sleepers, this lush harvest moon merely ushers in yet another night of anxiety and frustration. About one in three American adults claims to be a poor sleeper.

CHAPTER 2

WHAT CAUSES INSOMNIA?

Did you toss and turn the night before your big game—the one where you knew everyone would be counting on you to help capture the championship? What happened the night after your victory? Did you lie in bed wide awake and relive the action play by play?

Or do final exams keep you up at night? Remember how you moped around, lost your appetite, and barely slept when your big romance fizzled? Or how you were too keyed up to sleep the night after your first college admission letter arrived? Or maybe it was just being alone at home; you were too old to be scared of the dark, but what were all those strange noises?

These and other everyday situations involving emotional extremes, in which excitement or happiness on one side is contrasted with depression or anxiety on the other, are familiar triggers for insomnia in persons of all ages. Although the term insomnia literally means "no sleep," it is used by most people to describe trouble falling or staying asleep, almost always with the consequence of being unable to function as well as usual the following day. About one in three American adults says he or she is a poor sleeper, and one in six terms the problem serious.

Sleep specialists distinguish among three types of insomnia—transient, short-term, and chronic—and note that the possible causes of each are numerous.

Transient insomnia is the experience of a night or two of poor sleep. Probably everyone suffers from it now and then and thus knows that a little lost sleep has no lasting consequences. Indeed, sometimes people who miss sleep for reasons both pleasant and upsetting report that whatever they were focusing on consumed so much of their attention that they did not feel any ill effects of their sleep loss the next day. Often, however, people who experience a bad night complain of difficulty concentrating, weariness, and irritability the following day.

Merely sleeping in a strange bed may disrupt sleep; most people do not sleep quite as well as usual their first night away from home, whether it is under pleasant circumstances, such as a visit to a friend's house or a vacation, or under worrisome conditions, such as admission to a hospital. Rapid travel across many time zones upsets the inner clocks that regulate the timing of sleeping and waking. As a result, trouble in sleeping at night—as well as trouble in staying awake during the day—is a common symptom of "jet lag" and lasts roughly one to three days. Such brief illnesses as a cold or the flu or pains from sore muscles or an aching tooth may also make sleeping more difficult. In all of these instances, sleep usually improves within a few days.

Short-term insomnia involves sleep disturbances that last for two or three weeks. Here, ongoing stress at school, work, or home often is the reason: Worrying about grades, learning your parents are planning to divorce, or having a serious illness or death in the family are events that often trigger short-term insomnia. Although resolving such situations may take weeks or months, the passage of time usually fosters at least partial adjustment and brings sleep gradually back to its previous norm.

It is relatively easy to pinpoint the reasons for transient and short-term insomnia. That is less often the case for *chronic insomnia*, which may last for years, disrupting sleep every night, most nights, or several nights a month. The common experience of troubled sleep during troubled times has given rise to the erroneous belief that stress is behind most cases of chronic insomnia, too. Stress undoubtedly plays a key role, particularly for teenagers and persons in their twenties and thirties, but it is by no means the only culprit.

A nationwide study of 8,000 patients seeking treatment at sleep disorder centers shows that such physical problems as trouble in breathing or overactive leg muscles account for more than half of all cases of persistent insomnia. This startling finding makes sleep specialists emphasize that insomnia is not an illness, but a symptom, much like a fever or headache. As in the case of all good medical practice, insomnia, as a symptom, should be evaluated first before a decision about treatment is reached.

Many people experience mild to moderate anxiety about examinations. Transient insomnia, or a night or two of poor sleep, is a normal, if unpleasant, response to such stressful occasions.

Ongoing concern over money, schoolwork, or family problems can disrupt sleep for months or even years. Focusing on the cause of distress, rather than the insomnia itself, is the key to resolving sleep disturbances.

Causes of Chronic Insomnia

Studies of thousands of persons with chronic insomnia have identified numerous possible causes for the problem. Some of these are psychological, some have to do with personal habits, still others stem from physical disorders, and finally, genetic factors can also play a role.

Psychological Factors

•Vulnerability to insomnia: Some people tend to sleep poorly when under stress, much as others in similar situations suffer tension headaches or upset stomachs. Their insomnia may continue even after their stress has subsided. A 16-year-old who had the lead in his school play and also suffered from stage fright slept increasingly poorly as the performance date drew near. Despite the play's smooth presentation, he found he was not able to relax when he got into bed. He continued to worry about homework, dates, and even the fact that he could not sleep. Months later, he still took nearly an hour to fall asleep and woke up several times during the night. In this case, his family doctor suggested that he change his time for worrying from bedtime to a half hour right after dinner and learn progressive muscle relaxation techniques to use after turning out the lights. Soon afterward, his sleep improved.

•Persistent stress: People with persistent concerns about money, schoolwork, or family problems often sleep poorly. Talking with a psychological counselor may help a person to see these problems in a new light and manage them better. Focusing on the specific problem, rather than on the insomnia itself, is the key issue in resolving this type of sleep disturbance.

•Psychiatric problems: Chronic tension and anxiety may contribute to feeling "wound up" at bedtime and, thus, to difficulty in sleeping. Insomnia, particularly the type in which the sufferer awakens earlier than desired in the morning, is one of the most common symptoms of anxiety that may affect young children and adolescents as well as adults. People with clinical depression, schizophrenia, and other psychiatric disorders also may sleep poorly. Treatment of the underlying disorder, usually involving medication as well as psychotherapy, often improves sleep.

•Learned insomnia: People who do not sleep well when under stress often worry about the impact of poor sleep on their ability to function the next day. Often, they decide to try harder to sleep at night. But a willful effort to sleep often proves to have an effect opposite to what is desired. When people lie in bed wide awake, wishing they were asleep, their worries often escalate. They may soon begin mentally to link such bedroom activities as changing into a nightgown or pajamas or turning off the lights with staying awake instead of falling asleep. Those who learn to be insomniacs this way often fall asleep unintentionally, while reading the newspaper or watching television, or in less appropriate settings, such as on the living room couch or behind the wheel of a car. Even if they sleep poorly only a few times a month, they may continue to worry about their difficulty in sleeping. Techniques devised to remedy this type of insomnia focus on changing behavior that interferes with sleep and on overcoming worried thoughts. (See also Chapter 7.)

Personal Habits

•Use of stimulants: Caffeine, which is a mild stimulant, is perhaps the most widely used psychoactive drug in the world. A 12-ounce caffeine-containing soft drink has about 50 mg of caffeine, roughly the same amount as a cup of instant coffee or tea. Drinking a caffeine-containing beverage near bedtime usually prolongs the time it takes to fall asleep and can trigger awakening during the night. Because caffeine remains in the bloodstream for many hours and continues to have a stimulating effect, sleep specialists generally advise persons who are troubled by insomnia to avoid caffeine within four to six hours of bedtime.

Nicotine is a stimulant, too; smokers take longer to fall asleep and sleep more lightly than nonsmokers. Ingredients in many commonly used prescription and nonprescription drugs, including those for weight loss, asthma, and colds, also may disrupt sleep, a problem that the doctor can often remedy by changing the dosage or the time a particular medication is taken.

•Use of alcohol: A beer or glass of wine in the evening may help people relax and, as a result, find it easier to fall asleep. Before the 1960s, when effective drugs to aid sleep became widely available, doctors often suggested that persons with trouble falling asleep consume a modest amount of alcohol at bedtime. Recent research, however, shows that alcohol's value in inducing sleep is far outweighed by its ability to disrupt sleep later in the night, and doctors now generally advise against its use.

•Erratic hours: Staying up late on Friday and Saturday nights and sleeping late on Saturday and Sunday mornings disrupts sensitive body clocks that program the body to sleep at certain times and stay awake at others. Late nights at the start of the weekend may cause "Sunday night insomnia" and "Monday morning blahs," frequent problems for teenagers and others who lead active social lives, and ones that often interfere with school or work performance on Mondays. Work schedules that demand frequent changes in sleep patterns similarly undermine sleep. By contrast, regular hours help prevent insomnia.

•Sedentary behavior: People who are inactive during the day also seem to have a diminished ability to sleep at night.

This type of sleep disturbance is similar to the experience of being in bed with the flu or a cold and waking and dozing intermittently. Whereas teenagers seldom lead sedentary lives, adults who work in offices during the day, watch television in the evening, and fail to exercise may be more susceptible to insomnia. Similarly, many elderly persons lead highly inactive lives, particularly if their mobility is limited by illness, and suffer from sleeplessness as a result.

•Misuse or overuse of sleeping pills: Sleeping pills, whether prescribed or sold over the counter, may help insomnia if they are used carefully and in moderation. If used every night, however, sleeping pills cease to benefit sleep after a few weeks. Continued use may lead to tolerance, or a need to take larger doses to feel an effect, and dependence, or a psychological need for the medication. Discontinuing the use of sleeping pills, however, may lead to a temporary worsening of sleep disturbances. Problems associated with the use of sleeping pills are further detailed in Chapter 3.

Nicotine, the psychoactive drug in tobacco, is a powerful stimulant and can cause poor sleep. As a rule, smokers take longer to fall asleep and sleep more lightly than nonsmokers.

Noise pollution is a common cause of sleep disruption. Masking unwelcome sounds with "white noise" from an air conditioner or a fan can sometimes lead to better sleep.

Physical Disorders

Most physical disorders that disrupt sleep are rare in teenagers. They typically first appear in people in their forties and fifties and become increasingly common in old age. Interestingly, chronic insomnia is reportedly 8 times more common among women older than 40 than among men in the same age group. Various physical disorders are associated with chronic insomnia.

•Breathing disorders: Pauses in breathing during sleep (known as sleep apnea) may rouse a sleeper dozens, even hundreds, of times during a night. These pauses may last as little as 10 seconds, so brief a time that the sleeper does not remember them in the morning. But even brief interruptions contribute to the sense that sleep was light or restless. Sleep apnea may affect people who breathe normally when wide awake. Although 1 in 3 people aged 65 or older may experience some sleep apnea, generally the consequences are not serious and treatment is not indicated. However, they often are better off avoiding sleeping pills, because these drugs may further worsen breathing. For severe cases of sleep apnea, a new technique known as continuous positive airway pressure aids breathing by keeping the airway open during sleep.

•Periodic leg movements: Muscle contractions of the legs, which last only a second or two but recur about twice a minute for an hour or longer and can occur one or more times a night, may cause hundreds of unremembered arousals and a morning complaint of light sleep. Treatment includes medications, evening exercise, and warm baths.

•Waking brain activity in sleep: Some people maintain brain activity characteristic of wakefulness and do not fall fully asleep. They complain that their sleep is light or restless. This disorder was only recently identified, and its cause is still unknown.

•Reflux: Reflux occurs when stomach contents back up into the esophagus. If this happens when a person is awake and in an upright posture, swallowing a few times will rapidly clear the irritating materials away. But the usual sleeping posture, along with the normally lower frequency of swallowing in a sleeping state, increases the likelihood that the irritating materials will stay in contact with the esophagus for a longer time. Reflux may cause a person to awaken coughing and choking several times a night with pain or tightness in the midchest area. To prevent reflux, doctors often advise elevating the head of the bed on six- to eight-inch blocks. New medications to combat the condition are also available.

•Pain: Arthritis, angina, lower back injury, headache, and other disorders that cause pain during waking hours also disrupt sleep. A doctor may be able to suggest ways to ease these problems.

•Other illnesses: Many illnesses, and in particular those that affect the central nervous system (such as epilepsy and multiple sclerosis), may disrupt sleep. Insomnia, along with nightmares and troubled breathing during sleep, is a prominent symptom of the "post-polio" syndrome, a newly recognized condition that affects an estimated one fourth of those who developed polio in the 1940s and 1950s. Mountain climbers may experience insomnia as part of high-altitude sickness.

Genetic Factors

In much the same way that some people, like their parents or grandparents, are tall, smart, brown-eyed, or musically gifted, some people may be naturally good sleepers and others naturally poor sleepers. An extremely rare and incurable genetic disorder characterized by increasingly severe sleep disturbances invariably leads to death; known as Fatal Insomnia, it was recently observed and documented in three generations of an Italian family.

Unknown Causes

Sometimes no reason can be found to explain insomnia. Despite increasingly sophisticated tools for diagnosis, sleep specialists acknowledge that there is still a lot to learn.

Help for Insomnia

Because many cases of insomnia are triggered by such behaviors as consuming excessive caffeine or exercising too close to bedtime, personal detective work often suggests the appropriate remedial action. Insomnia that lasts three or four weeks or longer needs investigation by a family doctor, an internist, or a specialist at a sleep disorder center.

A doctor treating sleeplessness normally takes a medical history of the patient, performs a physical exam, and may order certain laboratory tests, such as those of hormone functions, to determine the reason for poor sleep. He or she may interview other members of the household to learn if a person snores loudly, thrashes around, walks while asleep, or has some other noteworthy behavior. The doctor will also assess the impact of insomnia on daily life by asking, for example, about depression or fatigue.

A person complaining of insomnia may sometimes benefit from information and education. Occasionally, a person who is satisfied with only five or six hours of sleep a night erroneously concludes something is wrong because of the common belief that everybody needs eight hours of sleep. The amount of sleep needed for a person to feel fully alert the next day varies considerably; national surveys show that 7 to 8 hours is merely the amount most people get, but numerous cases of adults who need as few as 2 or as many as 11 hours of sleep a night have been documented in sleep laboratories. Moreover, sleep laboratory studies show that many insomniacs actually get as much sleep as noninsomniacs; more crucial than the amount of sleep is the perception that sleep was unsatisfactory and the adverse impact of disturbed sleep on one's activities and mood the next day.

Sometimes the problem is not with sleep itself, but with its timing. Many people who cannot fall asleep until three or four o'clock in the morning label their problem "insomnia." They struggle to get out of bed in the morning, often needing two alarm clocks and cold showers to get moving. But if allowed to sleep until they awaken spontaneously, they are well rested. The practice of staying up late, common among college students, can reset the body's inner clocks. This internal readjustment generally presents a problem only when the students are at home for vacation and upset the household with their late hours, or after graduation, when they must

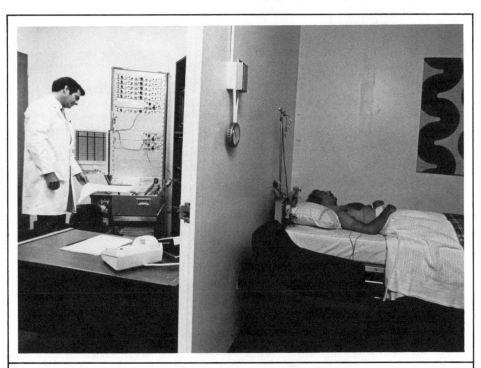

A sleep specialist monitors a patient at the Sleep Disorders Center at Columbia-Presbyterian Medical Center in New York City. Insomnia that lasts more than three or four weeks calls for investigation.

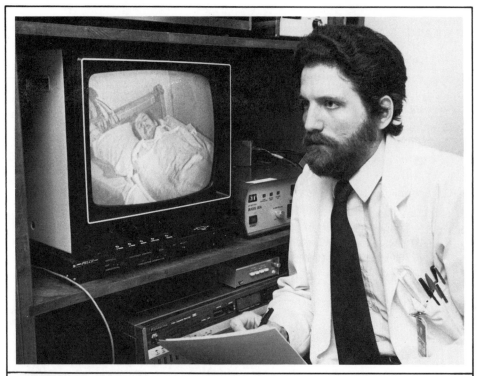

A sleep disorders specialist looks for clues to solve a case of serious insomnia. Sleep center evaluations include comprehensive physical and psychological examinations.

get to work earlier in the morning than they prefer. A treatment for resetting natural body clocks known as chronotherapy (literally, "time therapy"), usually overseen by a sleep specialist, involves staying up later and later on successive days, and consequently getting up later and later, until the desired bedtime is reached.

When poor sleep habits contribute to insomnia, the doctor may provide or suggest counseling. For some types of insomnia, the doctor may prescribe medication or advise further evaluation at a sleep disorder center.

Persons making an appointment at a sleep center are often asked to record their sleep and waking patterns for a week or two before their initial visit. The sleep center evaluation includes a comprehensive physical and psychological exam.

A person complaining of insomnia may also be asked to spend a night or two in the sleep evaluation laboratory, where sleep can be monitored. Sensors placed on forehead, scalp, outer corners of eyes, and elsewhere on the body enable the recording of brain waves, muscle activity, leg movements, breathing, heartbeat, and other bodily functions.

Sleep may be studied during the day as well as at night. A series of opportunities to nap every two hours, known as the Multiple Sleep Latency Test, assesses daytime sleepiness, which is often extreme when insomnia is severe.

After the evaluation is complete, counseling, medications, or other therapy may be recommended. Recent advances in understanding the many complicated reasons for insomnia enable today's sleep specialists to help most troubled sleepers.

A 19th-century country doctor doles out a medication to one of his patients. Many potions prescribed for sleep during this era were laced with opium, an addictive drug with no long-term therapeutic value in the treatment of insomnia.

CHAPTER 3

HOW SLEEPING PILLS WORK

According to Greek mythology, poppies and countless calming and sleep-inducing herbs bloomed by the entrance to the dark cave of Hypnos, the god of sleep. Hypnos handed out poppy stalks and herbs to both gods and humans, bringing them tranquility, sedation, and sleep and giving his name to the medical term for sleeping pills, hypnotics (sometimes called sedative/hypnotics).

Even though the juices of the poppy and herbal extracts, as well as wine and other alcoholic drinks, have continued to be employed to aid sleep for centuries, the limitations of their usefulness were well recognized. In Shakespeare's *Othello*, Iago observes:

> Not poppy, nor mandragora,
> Nor all the drowsy syrups of the world
> Shall ever medicine thee to that sweet sleep
> Which thou owedst yesterday.

Modern drugs for sleep, the chemical cousins of poppies and herbs, include chloral derivatives (drugs derived from the sedative chloral hydrate), introduced in the mid-1800s; barbiturates, which came into use around 1900; heterocyclic

A sculpted head of Hypnos, the god of sleep. According to Greek mythology, Hypnos distributed poppy stalks and herbs to both gods and humans in efforts to provide them with tranquility, sedation, and sleep.

compounds (used primarily to treat depression), introduced in the 1950s; benzodiazepines, used since the 1960s; and nonprescription commercial agents, sold over the counter.

The *Physicians' Desk Reference (PDR)*, an annually published guide to prescription drugs arranged by brand and generic (chemical) name, currently lists nearly 50 prescription drugs as "hypnotics," or "sedatives," and the *PDR for Nonprescription Drugs* lists about 10 sleep aids that are sold in pharmacies, supermarkets, and similar stores and are often referred to as over-the-counter, or OTC, drugs. Specific types of sleep-inducing agents are examined more closely in Chapter 4.

Patterns of Use

For a large part of this century, the notion that "there's a pill for every ill" was highly prevalent among both the general public and physicians. In the heyday of patent medicines, preparations to relieve insomnia often contained a hefty dose of opium or alcohol.

An article by the physician Norman Bridge entitled "Some Truths About Sleep," published in the *Journal of the American Medical Association* in 1906, highlighted the problem. Bridge noted that, "Great numbers of people in our modern life of high nervous tension are victims of insomnia, more now than ever before, and the number is apparently increasing very rapidly in certain communities. Drugs to produce sleep were never in such high demand, were never used so freely, both as a temporary expedient and as a daily habit, as now; and they are sold in vast quantities all over the nervous world, and used according to the whim of the sleepless, more often without than with the advice of physicians.

"Insomnia therefore is a favorite harvest field of the exploiter of 'patent' nostrums, for he well knows that, driven to desperation by sleeplessness, its victim is ready to do anything that promises relief; and if sleep comes as an effect of a drug he is ready to forgive other and perhaps resulting ills, that may in the end be worse than the insomnia." Though published almost a century ago, these charges sound quite contemporary.

Data on numbers of prescriptions written in the United States were first collected in 1964; that year there were nearly 33 million prescriptions for sleeping pills. Some 42 million prescriptions for sleeping pills, an all-time high, were written in 1971; nearly half of these were for barbiturates.

When barbiturates were first synthesized in 1863, they were hailed as "miracle drugs," because they were more effective in relieving both anxiety and insomnia than previously available drugs were. But their dangers eventually became apparent. Relatively small overdoses proved fatal; in 1963, 10% of the suicides in the United States involved barbiturates. Over the years, barbiturates have gotten a lot of bad press, especially after several celebrities, including Marilyn Monroe and Jimi Hendrix, died of overdoses.

The discovery of REM sleep in the 1950s was followed by a rapid growth in the understanding of the nature of sleep. This, coupled with the development of the safer benzodiazepines (also known as minor tranquilizers, among them, Valium and Librium) in the late 1950s, and studies of their impact on sleep in the 1970s, served to change physicians' prescribing habits for sleeping pills.

In 1982, the most recent year for which figures are available, physicians in the United States wrote 21 million prescriptions for sleeping pills, half of the all-time high in 1971. Further, by 1982, use of barbiturates had fallen dramatically and represented only 9% of all sleeping pill prescriptions. Two thirds were for benzodiazepines and the remainder for nonbenzodiazepine-nonbarbiturate sleeping pills. Moreover, instead of recommending sleeping pills for every-night use, physicians had begun to view them as a temporary solution, to be used much as someone with a broken leg might use a crutch, and thus had begun to prescribe smaller quantities for shorter times.

Although sleeping pills still are among the most widely prescribed drugs, and insomnia is a common health problem, a surprisingly small percentage of the population actually uses drugs for sleep. A major national survey in 1979 of U.S. adults

Marilyn Monroe at her effervescent best at a Golden Globe awards dinner in Hollywood. Monroe reportedly died from an overdose of barbiturates, a class of prescription drugs that is one of the leading causes of fatal drug poisoning.

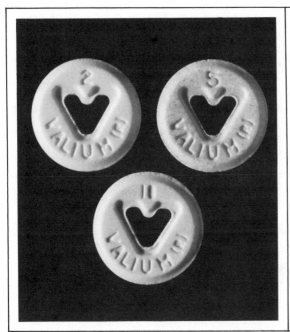

When taken under medical supervision, the widely prescribed tranquilizer Valium effectively relieves anxieties that are often the underlying cause of sleep disorders.

aged 18 to 79 who are not living in nursing homes or other institutions showed that insomnia afflicts 35% of all adults during the course of a year, and half of these people term their problem serious. But in the year prior to the survey, only 2.6% of this group had used a medically prescribed sleeping pill, according to researchers from the Institute for Research in Social Behavior in Oakland, California; the National Institute of Mental Health in Bethesda, Maryland; and the University of Chicago.

Most used the pills for only one or two nights at a time, or if they took pills regularly, for periods of less than two weeks. Only a small group of those who used sleeping pills at all — 11% of the users but only .3% of all subjects questioned—had used the drugs regularly for a year or longer.

The researchers also examined use of antianxiety and antidepression drugs, because these drugs have calming properties that often are useful in treating the sleep disorders that often accompany depression and anxiety. When the use of these drugs was also taken into account, only 4.3% of adults surveyed reported taking a drug prescribed for sleep. Some 3.1% had used a nonprescription (OTC) sleeping pill.

Former first lady Betty Ford discusses her recovery from addiction to medication she originally began taking for pain relief. Such addiction is a chronic danger when drug therapy is used in the treatment of pain, anxiety, or insomnia.

This survey found that women, who in general are more likely to seek medical advice and to take medication than men, were about twice as likely to use a prescription drug for sleep. It also found that older people used more medicines than younger ones; as was expected, they also had more health problems. Numerous studies show that 40% of those who use sleeping pills in the United States are aged 65 or older. This age group also receives 30% of all prescriptions, even though they represent only about 11% of the nation's population.

According to the survey, the majority of subjects with severe insomnia took no medication for sleep at all, leading the researchers to wonder what, if any, alternatives these people employ to obtain relief. They note, "We have found that negative attitudes toward drug therapy are widely prevalent in American society, and these attitudes probably contribute to the generally conservative use of drugs described above."

Of course, sleeping pills are generally given to about half of all patients in hospitals, prior to minor surgery or to painful diagnostic procedures. They are also given to many residents of nursing homes.

What Sleeping Pills Do

American comedian W. C. Fields once asserted, "All the insomniac needs is more sleep." This idea, coupled with the notion that substantially more sleep can be obtained with sleeping pills, is still widely held. But both concepts are wrong.

Insomnia is a complex disorder with many causes. Ideally, a sleeping pill would "cure" all that is wrong. Short of that, a sleeping pill should supply deep, restful sleep; treat the patient's specific complaints, such as trouble falling or staying asleep; remain effective for as long as it is used; improve alertness and mood the next day; not interact adversely with other drugs; be nonaddictive; be relatively safe; and not have negative aftereffects when its use is discontinued. How well do today's sleeping pills meet these goals?

•Effects on sleep: People who take a sleeping pill typically fall asleep 10 to 20 minutes faster and sleep 20 to 40 minutes

The elderly are often given sleeping pills for treatment of insomnia when other approaches, such as psychotherapy, relaxation techniques, or nutritional supplements, might be more effective.

longer than those who take no sleep aid. More important, the next morning they generally report feeling that they slept better than they do after a night without using a pill. However, their drug-induced sleep probably did not follow a normal pattern.

Sleeping pills reduce the deep sleep of stage 3-4 as well as the REM state in which vivid dreams usually occur. Even though scientists still do not know the purpose of the various sleep states and stages and have not proven that the changes induced by sleeping pills are harmful, most agree that tinkering with normal sleep is not "ideal." Ideally, a sleeping pill would help to normalize sleep.

•Effects on specific symptoms: Sleeping pills provide what doctors call "symptomatic relief." In general, this means that they may help a person to fall asleep faster, to wake less often during the night, and to sleep longer. But insomniacs have many complaints. They may say it takes too long to fall asleep, they wake too often during the night or too early in the morning, they do not feel well rested in the morning, and/or they are exhausted during the day. They also may have daytime problems of which they are unaware, such as slowed reaction time, diminished coordination, or an irritable mood. A person with insomnia complaints may even prove in the sleep laboratory to have what appears to be normal sleep.

Unfortunately, scientists are not able to target specific symptoms exclusively in studying the action of sleeping pills. Thus, they are faced with the problem of how to evaluate the effectiveness of these drugs, a task that involves both objective measurements, such as brain wave recordings during waking hours, and subjective measurements, such as questionnaires completed by the sleeping-pill user. Getting "more" sleep, by itself, is seldom enough to relieve a complaint of insomnia; indeed, "too much" sleep makes some people groggy.

Studies of sleeping pills usually involve comparisons of their effects on young adult insomniacs who meet certain criteria with those on young adult normal sleepers. The majority of sleeping pill users, however, are older adults, who tend to have more health problems and to take other medications. These factors may color the results of studies and make it difficult to extrapolate data on adults from the results of studies on young people.

•Duration of effectiveness: Sleeping pills, like other drugs, often are distinguished by their "elimination half-life," a mathematical concept that refers to the amount of time it takes to distribute half of the drug throughout the body and then to eliminate that amount from the system. This is not an indication of the span of a drug's action, but it is time that can be measured, and thus it allows comparisons between various drugs.

Sleeping pills generally are classified as short acting, intermediate acting, or long acting. These terms are relative. Drugs with different lengths of action aim to meet different needs. Shorter-acting drugs should prove most useful for persons whose primary complaint is trouble in falling asleep, and longer-acting drugs, for persons needing sedation during the day. Sleeping pills may, however, affect other behavior, such as the ability to remember, for a longer time than they affect sleep.

•Impact on alertness during the night: Once asleep, a person ordinarily expects to stay asleep. A drug that wears off too quickly might trigger awakenings. But sometimes a person awakens during the night needing to go to the bathroom or to respond to a crying child. If a person who has taken a sleeping pill must get out of bed during the night, the drug's effectiveness in reducing alertness becomes a serious drawback.

Elderly persons who awaken during the night, for example, are more prone to fall and possibly suffer fractures if they have taken sleeping pills. Thus, sleeping pills may be appropriate during a period of severe insomnia for an elderly person who can call on an aide; whereas sleeping pills may be a bad idea for an elderly person who lives alone.

•Impact on alertness the following day: A drug that wears off too slowly, causing drowsiness during waking hours, may make it harder to work effectively in school or at the office and particularly to undertake tasks that demand full alertness, such as operating machinery or driving. On the other hand, daytime drowsiness may be welcomed, for example, by someone recovering from surgery and confined to bed.

Unlike most drugs, which are designed to work around the clock, sleeping pills have an effect that goes from desirable to undesirable with the passage of time. Researchers reviewed the results of 52 studies of the effect of sleeping pills on people's ability to play video games, steer and brake driving simulators, sort cards, copy symbols, and carry out other tasks of coordination, reaction time, and memory the following day. They concluded that such drugs "generally improve the quality of sleep, but not the quality of daytime performance." Furthermore, the higher the dose, the worse the performance.

•Development of tolerance and dependence: The benefits of sleeping pills in inducing and maintaining sleep generally fade in just a few weeks. After taking them every night for two or three weeks, the user may notice that they are not working as well as they did previously. He or she may take longer to fall asleep and may experience more frequent awakenings during the night.

Recalling how helpful the drugs were initially, the user may be tempted to increase the dose. Much like the well-known brand of potato chips whose advertisement boasts, "You can't have just one," sleeping pills may prove equally seductive. The person may begin to need increasing quantities of the drug to experience the same effect; this need, called tolerance, is a characteristic of addiction. When the person continues to take the drug, even though the benefits have evaporated, it is a symptom of psychological dependence.

•Interaction with other drugs: Sleeping pills may interact with other depressant drugs, most notably alcohol, producing an effect greater than either would alone. Some sleeping pills produce this effect even if the pill is taken at bedtime and the alcohol is consumed late the following afternoon or even several days later. The individual's response to multiple drug ingestion may have serious consequences in some settings. Impaired coordination can make driving, for example, a risky activity.

Sleeping pills also may interfere with the way the body absorbs or uses other drugs, including those used for duodenal ulcers, heart disease, and depression. If a person is taking any drugs — including those purchased without a prescription — it is always wise to seek the advice of a physician or pharmacist about possible drug interactions.

•Adverse effects on other illnesses or medical conditions: Sleeping pills may pose a danger to some insomniacs, as in the case of those who experience pauses in breathing, because these drugs may make breathing even more shallow. Many people are not aware that they have trouble breathing

Physical therapy for a seven-year-old girl whose mother took the sleeping aid thalidomide during her pregnancy. Use of this drug in Europe led to the birth of more than 5,000 deformed infants before it was withdrawn from the market.

during sleep and thus unwittingly may put themselves at risk. Sleeping pills also increase heart rate during sleep, a potential hazard for people afflicted with heart disease.

No sleeping pills have been determined to be safe for use by pregnant women. (Most other drugs, including alcohol, are unsafe as well.) Use of one particular sleeping agent, thalidomide, by pregnant women in West Germany and other European countries, as well as in Canada, led to the birth of more than 5000 children without arms and legs between 1959 and the early 1960s, before the cause of these tragic birth defects was identified and the drug was withdrawn from the world market in 1962. Test marketing of thalidomide in the United States was linked to deformities in at least nine infants; approval of the drug in the United States was forestalled by the vigilance of Frances Kelsey, a Food and Drug Administration (FDA) physician. Her action led to the passage of new laws strengthening safety requirements for new prescription drugs and requiring that new drugs be proved effective as well as safe.

Women who are breast-feeding may pass on small amounts of any medication they are taking to the baby. Thus, drug use by nursing mothers should be supervised by a physician.

Recent studies suggest benzodiazepines may alter memory, specifically, the memory of events occurring after the pill is taken. They also may interfere with reaction time and activities requiring alertness the next day.

•Effects of overdoses: Ideally, there is a large difference between the dosage needed to fulfill a drug's indicated purpose and the amount that would be fatal, if an overdose were consumed. Overdoses may occur deliberately, as in the case of an individual attempting suicide, or accidentally, as in the case of a child who thinks the pretty pills in grandma's medicine cabinet are candy. The margin of safety for barbiturates is low; for benzodiazepines, it is high. Nonetheless, an overdose of benzodiazepines still may cause a variety of serious reactions, including confusion and coma.

•Problems that emerge after pill use is stopped: A person who stops taking sleeping pills may experience what appears to be a resurgence in insomnia, sometimes referred to as "rebound insomnia," which involves sleeping problems that are as bad as, or even worse than, those that existed before the use of pills started. Some researchers believe this problem reflects the body's physical dependence on the pills and is in fact a symptom of withdrawal from the drug.

Another symptom sometimes experienced by people no longer using sleeping pills is an abundance of anxiety-filled dreams. One hypothesis attributes this response to the suppressive action of sleeping pills on the REM state in which most vivid dreams occur, thus triggering a "REM rebound" when they are withdrawn. This problem seems to be minimized when the use of sleeping pills is stopped gradually.

These are among the issues that prompted a panel of experts at a conference on drugs and insomnia, which was held in 1983 by the National Institutes of Health and the National Institute of Mental Health, to agree that "treatment of insomnia should start with the assessment and necessary correction of sleep hygiene and habits," and that "sleeping pills, when appropriate, should be only part of a comprehensive treatment plan that might also include advice on good sleep habits and psychotherapy."

The rest of this book examines the key components of a comprehensive insomnia treatment plan, starting with a look at when sleeping pills may be appropriate and the different types of drugs that are available today.

Shift workers at a Detroit automobile plant head for home. People whose work hours change back and forth between daytime and nighttime shifts frequently suffer from transient insomnia.

CHAPTER 4

SLEEPING PILLS: USES AND TYPES

A decision to use any drug involves weighing the advantages against the drawbacks. Ideally, the benefits far outweigh the disadvantages. Sleeping pills may be appropriate when a person has experienced a few nights of poor sleep or anticipates sleeplessness. There are several forms of insomnia that may, under certain circumstances, be appropriately treated with sleeping pills.

Transient Insomnia

Transient insomnia — a few nights of bad sleep — can be caused by a number of different factors. Air travel, for example, across many time zones upsets internal body clocks, causing jet lag. Prominent symptoms include both insomnia and daytime sleepiness. Although it takes about one day for each time zone crossed to reset all of these internal clocks, sleep usually starts to improve after one to three nights. Taking a sleeping pill on those nights may hasten this improvement, with the result that the user will feel less sleepy during the daytime. Taking a sleeping pill on the flight itself is not recommended, because it might interfere with a person's

The Concorde takes off from New York's Kennedy Airport. Air travel across many time zones upsets internal body clocks and causes jet lag, symptoms of which include insomnia and daytime sleepiness.

ability to react in an emergency. Once in the new time zone, adjustment is facilitated by following the premise, "When in Rome, do as the Romans do" — that is getting up at about the same hour each day, regularizing nightly sleep hours, and keeping active during the day.

Shift workers are also vulnerable to transient insomnia. People whose hours on the job change radically, often switching back and forth between daytime and nighttime shifts, experience the same symptoms as jet travelers. They find it hard to stay awake when they would rather be asleep and hard to sleep when they would rather be awake. Travelers who are immersed completely in a new time zone can adjust more easily, because daily routines — bed time, wake up time, and meal times — are quickly reestablished according to their normal patterns. Shift workers, however, may have to eat breakfast at 11 o'clock at night or sleep while it is bright outside. Their sleep may be disrupted by daytime traffic noises, sounds of children playing, even the ringing of the phone. Because shift workers want to spend time with their families and friends on weekends and days off, they often go back to an up-during-the-day, asleep-at-night schedule, further disrupting their inner clocks. Researchers suggest that shift workers may benefit from using sleeping pills for one to three nights after a shift change.

Finally, periods of acute stress can wreak havoc on sleep patterns. Whereas most people are not unduly troubled by a night or two of bad sleep, those who are prone to insomnia may sleep easier if they take sleeping pills during a personal

A traffic officer on duty in New York City. Job-related stress is a common culprit in moderate to serious cases of insomnia.

or work crisis. The pills may keep "poor sleep" from being added to the list of things they are worrying about, and indeed, sleeping restfully may enable them to cope better with the particular stress.

Short-term Insomnia

Continuing stress can often cause short-term insomnia, lasting perhaps as long as three weeks. Anxiety over adjusting to a new school or starting a new job and grief following a death in the family often lead to poor sleep. And, of course, sleeping poorly may make it even harder to function effectively during the day. Thus, use of sleeping pills for up to three weeks — not necessarily every night but usually after a night or two of bad sleep — may help keep temporary insomnia from becoming chronic. Because taking a sleeping pill in the middle of the night is more likely to cause a hangover the next day than taking a pill at bedtime, many doctors advise planning in advance whether a pill is to be taken on a particular night. Or the doctor may caution against taking a pill after a certain hour; however, shorter-acting pills are less likely to cause next-day drowsiness, even if taken at one or two o'clock in the morning. A person who cannot sleep may be advised to try specific behavioral techniques described in Chapter 7 or to "tough it out" until the next day, because the consequences of a little lost sleep are generally not severe.

Chronic Insomnia

If people who are prone to insomnia can anticipate problems sleeping — for example, in the face of having to give a speech or take an overnight trip — they may use a sleeping pill as a preventive strategy. Again, the pills would not be used every night, but only after a night or two of poor sleep. Some sleep specialists suggest that merely having sleeping pills in the medicine cabinet may reduce anxiety about not sleeping and thus reduce the need for their use.

Panelists at the 1983 national consensus conference on drugs and insomnia concluded, "When pharmacotherapy [treatment with drugs] is indicated, benzodiazepines are preferable." They also emphasized, "Patients should receive the smallest effective dose for the shortest clinically necessary

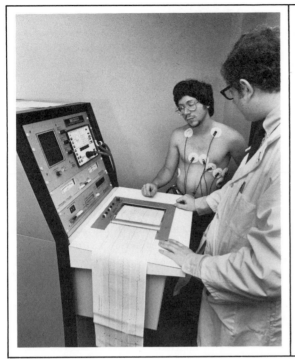

A man undergoes a stress test for heart trouble. In cases of chronic insomnia, any possible underlying physical disorder should be investigated.

period of time; this recommendation applies especially to the elderly." The panel added, "The choice of a specific drug should be based upon its pharmacological properties in conjunction with the particular clinical situation and needs of the patient."

Sleep Medications

There are several specific types of both prescription and non-prescription drugs available today to help people sleep.

Benzodiazepines

Two thirds of all sleeping pills prescribed in the United States today are members of the chemical family known as benzo-diazepines, also known as minor tranquilizers. According to *Drug Evaluations* (6th edition, 1986), the standard reference guide on drugs published by the American Medical Association, benzodiazepines are usually the drugs of choice to improve sleep, to relieve anxiety, or to bring about sedation.

Benzodiazepines are among the most widely prescribed drugs in the United States.

All sleeping pills are depressant drugs; that is, they slow the activity of the brain and central nervous system. Although the site in the brain at which benzodiazepines work and their mechanism of action are matters of speculation, the most likely hypothesis is that they enhance the effects of the major inhibitory neurotransmitter, gamma-aminobutyric acid (GABA). (A neurotransmitter is a chemical that carries chemical "messages" between nerve cells.) GABA, which is found in the brain and the spinal cord, acts to reduce the activity of the nerves that it contacts.

The benzodiazepines most commonly used to treat insomnia include triazolam (Halcion), which has a mean half-life of 2.6 hours; temazepam (Restoril), which has a mean half-life of 14.7 hours; and flurazepam (Dalmane), which has a mean half-life of 74 hours in young males and 90 in young females. None of these is available generically. A new benzodiazepine, quazepam, has recently been approved for the treatment of insomnia. Other members of the benzodiazepine

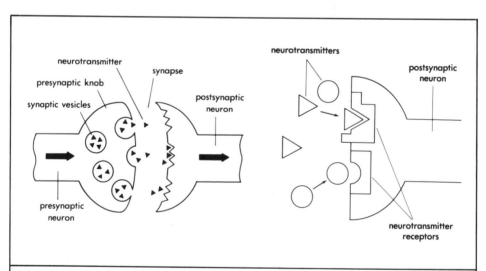

The drawing on the left shows how one neuron signals another across the synapse between them by emitting neurotransmitters. The illustration on the right shows how each kind of neurotransmitter fits only one kind of receptor on the target neuron.

family, such as diazepam (Valium), oxazepam (Serax), and lorazepam (Ativan) are effective sleep aids, according to the AMA guide.

The differences in the half-lives of the benzodiazepines most commonly used to induce sleep lead to different indications for their use. Triazolam is most effective for people who have difficulty in falling asleep, whereas temazepam and flurazepam are preferable for those who experience difficulty in staying asleep. The shorter half-lives of triazolam and temazepam make them less likely to interfere with alertness and manual dexterity the following day; however, sleep specialists debate whether they are effective long enough to sustain sleep through the night. The longer half-life of flurazepam makes it more likely to produce daytime carry over and thus more suitable when illness or anxiety make daytime sedation desirable. When taken several nights in a row, its level of concentration in the blood rises until it eventually reaches what is called a "steady state."

The half-lives of the various benzodiazepines are prolonged in the elderly because of age-related reductions in the body's ability to break down and excrete drugs. Some benzodiazepines, including those with a high attraction to fat cells, are burned more rapidly in men because men have a lower proportion of fat to total body weight than women. The half-life of diazepam is prolonged in users of low-dose estrogen-containing oral contraceptives (birth control pills).

A key reason the use of benzodiazepines has superceded that of barbiturates is that an overdose of a benzodiazepine has a higher margin of safety than that of a barbiturate. If an excess dose of benzodiazepam is taken in conjunction with alcohol, however, the safety factor is considerably reduced.

Some benzodiazepines have been reported to have an effect on memory that persists beyond their effect on sleep, a matter of considerable active investigation. In one study, a group of healthy young adults took either a benzodiazepine or a placebo (a nonactive look-alike) at bedtime. The next day they were asked to listen to and remember a list of words; all could recall the list satisfactorily. However, 8 and 24 hours later, those who took the benzodiazepines remembered fewer words than those who did not. Some did not even remember hearing the list.

Barbiturates

The three barbiturates prescribed as hypnotics are amobarbital (Amytal), with a mean elimination half-life of 25 hours; pentobarbital (Nembutal), with a mean half-life of 15 to 50 hours; and secobarbital (Seconal), with a mean half-life of 28 hours. Generic forms are also available. Like benzodiazepines, barbiturates are thought to enhance the effects of the inhibitory neurotransmitter GABA.

Barbiturates in doses used for sleep commonly produce a "hangover" the following day and increased drowsiness. Thus, persons using them need to be cautioned about such activities as driving that require alertness, judgment, and physical coordination.

According to the AMA, barbiturates remain one of the leading causes of fatal drug poisoning, many cases of which are suicides. When taken in conjunction with alcohol, the danger is increased. Barbiturates may also interact adversely with many other drugs, including those used to treat depression and pain. In addition, barbiturates have a high addictive potential. If a person dependent upon barbiturates stops using the drug, he or she may suffer such unpleasant withdrawal symptoms as tremors, convulsions, and hallucinations.

Nonbenzodiazepines-Nonbarbiturates

Compounds in this category have also been largely replaced by benzodiazepines because of concerns about their safety, as well as problems associated with their use, such as gastric irritation.

Chloral hydrate (Noctec; also available in generic forms), which has a mean half-life of four to nine and one-half hours, is particularly useful for persons who have difficulty falling asleep, and, according to the AMA, may be the most preferred of the nonbenzodiazepine sleep aids.

Others in this category include ethinamate (Valmid), ethchlorvynol (Placidyl), glutethimide (Doriden; also available in generic forms), and methyprylon (Noludar). Like chloral hydrate, these have a rapid onset and a brief duration of action; their overall safety is said to be comparable to the barbiturates.

Nonprescription Sleep Aids

Sleeping pills that can be bought without prescription — often referred to as over-the-counter, or OTC, drugs — are used more widely than prescription sleep aids, particularly by persons under age 45, who generally have fewer illnesses and see doctors less often than people who are older.

OTC sleep aids get their drowsiness-inducing effect from antihistamines, substances also used in cold and allergy remedies, where drowsiness generally is considered an unwelcome side effect. They include diphenhydramine (Nervine, Nytol, Sleep-Eze 3, Sominex 2; also available in generic form), doxylamine (Unisom), and pyrilamine (Dormarex; also available in generic form); all have a mean elimination half-life of 9.3 hours.

The target symptom of these preparations is trouble in falling asleep; however, they may also help to maintain sleep. Like many prescription sleep aids, they may cause sleepiness and other effects that worsen the ability to drive or handle complex mental tasks the next day. They also may interact adversely with other drugs, including alcohol. Thus, they should be used with care.

Alcohol

The widespread use of alcohol at bedtime is enshrined in the familiar reference to it as a "nightcap." It was, in fact, once recommended as a sleep aid, but no longer. Scientists now recognize that the breakdown by the body of alcohol during sleep intensifies its REM stages, which in turn may cause disturbing dreams, numerous awakenings, and the perception in the morning of a restless night. Moreover, alcohol is addictive; even medicinal use of the drug can result in dependence.

L-tryptophan

This essential amino acid, one of the basic building blocks of protein, is a precursor (a chemical that is later converted to another form) of the brain chemical serotonin, which is believed to play a role in inducing and maintaining sleep. It occurs naturally in milk, meat, fish, poultry, eggs, beans, pea-

There is evidence that L-tryptophan, an essential amino acid that is found naturally in milk and other sources of protein, may have sleep-inducing properties.

nuts, and leafy green vegetables, and it has made its way into health food stores and drug stores in tablet form. Sleep laboratory studies suggest that it may help persons fall asleep faster. It is sold as a sleep aid in Europe, but still lacks FDA approval as a sleep aid in the United States, though approved as a "dietary supplement." (See also Chapter 5.)

Aspirin

This staple of the family medicine cabinet was proved in sleep laboratory studies to help people who have trouble staying asleep. Two aspirins at bedtime was the dose used. Aspirin may indirectly benefit sleep by reducing pain from chronic illnesses such as arthritis or by relieving temporary aches and pains that interfere with sleep.

Melatonin

Melatonin is a hormone manufactured by the pineal gland, which is connected to the nerve that carries information about light from the eye to the brain. When sunlight disappears, the production of melatonin soars. Among its other effects, this hormone appears to help people sleep. When healthy volunteers were given doses of melatonin during the afternoon, they all felt sleepy. These results suggest that melatonin could have a place in medicine as a sleep-promoting agent. Other studies have found that the administration of melatonin to travelers departing for another continent has greatly reduced their susceptibility to jet lag.

Other Drugs that Affect Sleep

Drugs used for a variety of medical and psychiatric disorders may benefit sleep, or, conversely, their side effects may cause disturbed sleep at night or excessive sleepiness during the day. Some common examples are as follows:

•Drugs often prescribed to relieve anxiety or depression are, as noted above, benzodiazepines; because of their sedative effects, doctors often advise patients to take a dose at bedtime. Such drugs include diazepam (Valium, Valrelease), lorazepam (Ativan), and alprazolam (Xanax). The difference between benzodiazepine drugs prescribed primarily for anxiety or depression and those prescribed primarily for sleep is essentially a matter of their sedative effect, with the more sedating drugs used mostly at night when sedation is desirable and the less sedating drugs used mostly during the day, when sedation usually is unwelcome.

•Drugs used for the common cold or asthma often contain antihistamines; the daytime drowsiness sometimes associated with their use is generally unwelcome. Still other decongestants, such as ephedrine sulphate, have the opposite effect, triggering alertness that can keep a person awake at night. Some drugs, such as the asthma medications theophylline and aminophylline, resemble caffeine in their chemical structure as well as in their propensity to disrupt sleep.

•Drugs used to reduce appetite, popularly called "diet pills," sometimes contain stimulants and thus may cause insomnia.

•Drugs used primarily as stimulants include amphetamine, methylphenidate, and pemoline. Such drugs have an important use in sleep disorder medicine in the treatment of narcolepsy, a disorder that often first appears during the late teens, in which unwanted sleep intrudes into and overwhelms normal wakefulness.

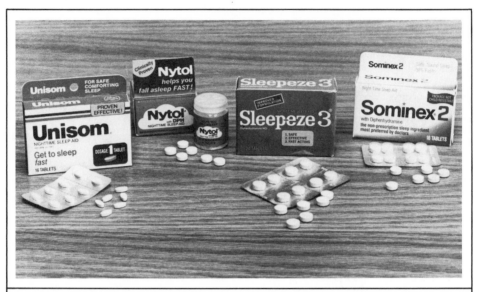

A number of preparations for the treatment of insomnia can be obtained without a prescription, but it is wise to consult your doctor before taking any of them and to follow package directions carefully.

Narcolepsy's most common symptom is a "sleep attack," in which the person falls asleep suddenly, often at inappropriate times. Sleep attacks frequently are triggered by intense emotion such as humor, anger, fear, or surprise; a student with narcolepsy may slump to his desk in sleep when a teacher calls on him in class or fall to the ground on hearing a joke. Sleep attacks may occur while crossing a busy street or driving; thus they may endanger the individual with narcolepsy or others.

Stimulants can help the person with narcolepsy to stay more alert; their use is combined with such behavioral treatments as regularly scheduled naps and sufficient sleep at regular hours at night. Stimulants have many drawbacks when used on a regular basis, as would be the case in the treatment of a chronic disease such as narcolepsy. People may develop tolerance, causing the need for larger and larger doses, and they may grow dependent on the drugs. Close monitoring by a physician is required, and stimulants often are advised for use only when maximum alertness is desired, as at school or work and while going to and from these sites, with "drug holidays" on weekends or days off. Stimulants are also used in the treatment of depression, attention-deficit disorder (formerly called "hyperactivity" because of a symptom now recognized often to be only part of the problem or not present at all), obsessive-compulsive disorder, and several other psychiatric conditions. Even when properly used, stimulants may trigger jitteriness, irritability, and insomnia. Unfortunately, they are also frequently abused in an attempt to avoid or overcome fatigue, elevate mood, or simply "get high." Sometimes, users attempt to compensate for the resulting insomnia by using depressants such as alcohol or sleeping pills.

•Drugs known as beta blockers, which are used for persons with heart disease, may have both sleep-inducing and sleep-disturbing effects. Indeed, in treating a patient with heart disease, a doctor must balance the beneficial and unwanted effects of a variety of drugs on a variety of bodily functions. Drugs such as diuretics, for example, that ease the strain on the heart may worsen breathing and consequently disturb sleep.

•Drugs known as corticosteroids, which are used to treat several inflammatory illnesses, including arthritis and lupus, increase alertness and therefore can trigger insomnia.

•Ribavirin, an experimental new drug used to treat an early form of infection caused by the AIDS virus, has insomnia, as well as irritability, among its side effects.

Side effects of legal drugs that occur frequently, such as insomnia or daytime drowsiness, are reported to manufacturers and the FDA and thus become part of the information a physician will review and take into account when prescribing medication. Although street drugs are sometimes loosely described as "uppers" or "downers," without controls there is no reliable way to determine their contents or predict their effects. The best way to minimize the likelihood of suffering adverse drug effects is to take only those drugs that are medically necessary and to let your doctor know all the drugs you are using.

All foods can be broken down into simple chemical compounds. Some of these chemicals can have druglike effects on the brain, influencing mood, behavior, and sleep patterns.

CHAPTER 5

FOOD AND MOOD

In the grocery store checkout line, you have probably let your gaze wander over the contents of other people's carts. No two are ever completely alike, and often, they lack even a single item in common. Given the thousands of food items in a typical supermarket and the hundreds of thousands of possible combinations, let alone the amounts consumed and the times they are eaten, it is no surprise that studies of the impact of foods on moods and behavior are so complex.

Yet all foods, whether naturally grown or concocted in a laboratory, are made of chemicals. These eventually enter the brain, where, like psychoactive drugs, they may influence moods and behavior. This notion is an old one; the ancient Egyptians, for example, ate onions in the hope of inducing sleep. The Greek physician Hippocrates noted some 2,400 years ago, "Let thy food be thy medicine and thy medicine be thy food."

Certain foods contain precursors for either the chemicals that the brain uses to convey information (neurotransmitters) or chemicals that alter the release of the neurotransmitters. Of special interest are neurotransmitters that are thought to influence alertness (dopamine and norepinephrine) and sleep (serotonin).

The Greek physician Hippocrates noted more than 2,400 years ago, "Let thy food be thy medicine and thy medicine be thy food."

Scientists at the Massachusetts Institute of Technology (MIT) report finding that when the brain is actively using dopamine and norepinephrine, people say they think faster and feel more energetic. The MIT researchers say that, by contrast, serotonin makes people feel less tense and better able to focus on the task at hand; at some times of the day, it may make people sleepy.

How Foods May Affect the Brain

The MIT research group suggests that, in order to produce dopamine and norepinephrine, the brain needs tyrosine, an amino acid and thus a basic "building block" of protein foods such as fish or chicken. To make serotonin, the brain needs tryptophan, another amino acid and also a basic constituent of protein foods. MIT researchers report that although eating protein foods boosts the amount of tyrosine in the brain, it does not seem to affect the amount of tryptophan in quite the same way.

They postulate the existence of a kind of chemical horse race in which the consumption of protein foods raises not only the levels of tyrosine and tryptophan, but also those of four other amino acids, all of which jockey for entrance into the brain. For some as yet unexplained reason, protein boosts the levels of the competing amino acids even higher than the level of tryptophan. Thus, the MIT team says, eating high-protein foods serves in fact to lower brain tryptophan levels.

Here, they report, carbohydrates, in the form of sweets and starches, can come to the rescue, by a somewhat indirect route. Eating carbohydrates stimulates the production of the hormone insulin; insulin in turn lowers the levels of the amino acids that compete with tryptophan, thereby leaving the field clear for it to gallop into the brain.

Not all researchers in the field agree with the above scenario. They note that the changes that purportedly occur after eating certain foods may be slight and subtle, making the theory hard to confirm; your age, sex, medicines you are taking, and other factors may alter the impact any foods might have. Yet many describe this theory as provocative and imaginative and call for replication of research and further study. At the same time, they caution that it is premature to suggest major dietary changes on the basis of the present findings.

Although all the evidence is clearly not yet in, several recent studies, using everyday foods, seem to support the hypothesis. Practical applications of the theory have been widely reported in magazines, books for the general public, and other media. The popular appeal is understandable; the notion that you can make major improvements in your life simply by food selection is highly alluring.

There probably is no harm in seeing whether consuming certain foods in a certain order at certain times of the day makes any difference in your motivation and performance, particularly because the suggested foods are most likely already part of your diet and tend to be low in fat, though not necessarily low in calories.

Power Meals

The basic strategy for an active day without midafternoon drowsiness, a relaxed evening, and restful sleep calls for eating high-protein meals during the day to promote alertness, and a high-carbohydrate evening meal and bedtime snack to promote sleepiness. It reportedly does not take much food in either category to have the desired effect — only three to four ounces of a protein food and one to one and a half ounces of a carbohydrate food. Typical meals and snacks contain larger quantities.

If you wish to adopt a power diet, eat a breakfast of plain yogurt with fresh fruit. Have a light lunch of three to five ounces of chicken or fish; a sandwich is fine. If you want to keep going after dinner, have protein foods and only a moderate amount of carbohydrates, but if you want to unwind in the evening, reverse the proportions; have pasta as your main course. Concentrate on carbohydrates in a bedtime snack; a toaster waffle with maple syrup is one suggestion. The rationale for this approach is described in more detail and accompanied by meal plans in a book written by MIT researcher Judith Wurtman, listed in the further reading section at the end of this book.

A supermarket checkout line. Studies concerning the effects of food on sleep suggest that high-protein foods promote alertness and carbohydrate-rich foods enhance relaxation.

Tryptophan Tablets

Sleep laboratory research also suggests that tryptophan in tablet form, in doses of 1 to 15 grams — roughly 1 to 15 times the amount in foods composing a typical American evening meal — may speed the time it takes to fall asleep in people for whom sleeplessness is a problem.

Taking tryptophan in tablet form eliminates competition from the other amino acids that are also present in foods and thus theoretically enhances speedy access by tryptophan to the brain. A recent review of studies concerning tryptophan found that for persons who have trouble falling or staying asleep, the benefits of tryptophan took some time to appear and in some cases appeared after the tryptophan was stopped. This delayed response has given rise to a treatment regimen known as "interval therapy," in which periods of tryptophan ingestion alternate with periods of nonuse.

The various studies found that tryptophan did not seem to have side effects and tolerance did not develop with long-term use; it also did not cause problems the next day with coordination, thinking, or memory. Further research is needed, however. No one knows the eventual effect of consuming this substance in doses much larger than would normally be consumed in the diet; animal studies show a connection between tryptophan use and the later development of bladder cancer.

The Effect of Caffeine

Caffeine is unquestionably a stimulant drug, and although scientists continue to investigate possible dangers, the current consensus is that caffeine taken in moderation — two cups of brewed coffee, four standard cola drinks or their equivalents, per day — appears to have no harmful long-term effects in most people.

The mean half-life of caffeine is about 5 to 6 hours in an adult, 12 hours in a user of birth-control pills, and 3.5 hours in a smoker. Thus, adults who have decided to restrict themselves to two cups of coffee a day can get the maximum benefits of alertness by having one cup first thing in the morning and the other in the midafternoon. The length of caffeine's half-life explains why it can interfere with sleep if it is consumed in the evening.

There is, however, substantial variability in how sensitive people are to caffeine, which explains why some people say that caffeine in the evening ruins their sleep, and others say it does not. (See Chapter 2.)

Caffeine may not have much of an alerting effect if you are already wide awake; when you are tired, its "pick-me-up" benefits are most noticeable. And caffeine will not make you more alert than you would be in your normal well-rested state; it helps restore you to alertness after fatigue sets in.

Package labels state the presence of caffeine in a product, but not its quantity; the latter may vary considerably, depending, for example, on the size of a "heaping" teaspoon of instant coffee you put into your cup, how big the cup is, or if tea is the beverage, how long it steeps. Caffeine-containing soft drinks have on the average about 50 mg of the substance. Thus, many young children and teenagers can consume at least as much caffeine in a day as the harried office worker who is frequently depicted as the typical coffee drinker. Coffee does account for roughly three quarters of the caffeine consumed in the United States today; the rest is found not only in soft drinks but also in tea, chocolate, and certain medications.

Since its discovery about 1,000 years ago, caffeine has been most often available in beverage form. Soft drinks, introduced about 100 years ago, were originally advertised as a new way to obtain caffeine; they took their name, "colas," from the caffeine-containing kola nut from which they were made. However, about 90% of the caffeine in present-day cola drinks is added in the manufacturing process. Advertisements for a new soft drink, Jolt Cola, return to the original concept and boast that it has twice the caffeine of Coke and Pepsi. The drink is available in most states.

In moderate doses, caffeine is not considered "a drug of abuse," as, for example, amphetamines are. A fatal overdose of caffeine would require rapid consumption of perhaps 200 cans of the typical caffeine-containing soft drink; hence, unlike most drugs, its potential for overdose usually is not a matter for concern. However, pills and capsules containing as much as 10 times the amount of caffeine in a typical caffeine-containing soft drink are sold by mail order firms, and they are potentially dangerous. They look like amphetamines and other drugs sold on the street as "speed" and thus find

Jolt Cola boasts that it contains more than twice the amount of caffeine found in other soft drinks. Although caffeine is a stimulant drug, it does not have any long-term side effects in most people if taken in moderation.

a ready market in teenagers and others looking for an easy "high." Deaths have been reported in people who swallowed a handful at a time; indeed, these drugs were blamed for more than a dozen deaths in 1980 and 1981.

Cutting back on coffee may trigger withdrawal symptoms such as severe headache; to avoid such problems, anyone who decides to reduce his or her daily intake should do so gradually.

Diet and Mental Illness

Excessive caffeine consumption — on the order of 7 to 10 or more cups of coffee a day — has been linked with the development of anxiety, even in healthy persons. And in persons diagnosed as having panic disorders, caffeine may produce even more anxiety, nervousness, fear, nausea, and restlessness. Doctors suggest that patients with panic disorders avoid

A bone-chilling winter morning in Oslo, Norway. People who suffer from winter depression, or seasonal affective disorder, often experience increased appetite, particularly for carbohydrates.

caffeine. The finding that caffeine exacerbates or even causes anxiety is giving scientists a new way of looking at the biological underpinnings of this disorder.

Increased appetite, particularly for carbohydrates, often resulting in weight gain along with excessive fatigue and time spent asleep, are among the symptoms of another psychiatric disorder, winter depression. Also called seasonal affective disorder, or SAD, it is most common for the symptoms to worsen in winter and improve dramatically in summer. Many people report suffering from the "winter blues," but SAD patients feel them more than most. The recognition that this type of depression comes on with the shortening of days in the fall and winter and lifts with the lengthening of days in the spring and summer has led to a new treatment: exposure to bright artificial lights during the fall and winter months that, in essence, bypasses these seasons and makes spring come early.

This and other research also suggests that not only is it possible that foods may affect our moods, but also that our moods may affect the foods we choose. People with SAD are not the only ones who crave high-carbohydrate "junk foods" when they are feeling down; many people report that sweets give them a boost. Such cravings are common in many women before their menstrual periods. Carbohydrates thus may sometimes serve as a mild tranquilizer.

Although much research needs to be done to clarify further the connections among food, mood, and behavior, it seems that there may be some truth to the old adage, "You are what you eat."

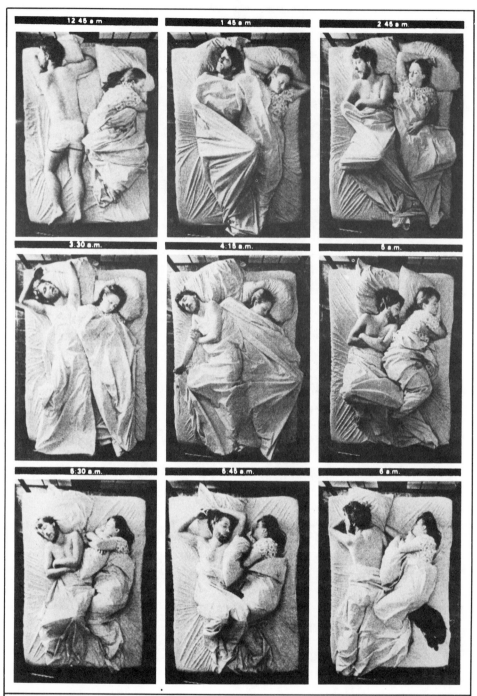

Even untroubled sleep involves some tossing and turning. A camera captured the movements of this couple during a normal, restful night.

CHAPTER 6

GOOD SLEEP HABITS

An article that appeared in the *Journal of the American Medical Association* in 1906 — shortly after barbiturates began to be used as hypnotics — said of such drugs, "While their use may be justified by an occasional exigency, they are in the main mischievous because, if for no other reason, they undertake a function and do a thing for the body that good hygiene and a better course of living, as a rule, should make unnecessary."

Such terms as "good hygiene" and "a better course of living" may sound stuffy, old-fashioned, and vague. In fact, they cover specific concepts that make eminent good sense even in today's world. These concepts were endorsed by the 1983 Federal Consensus Panel on Drugs and Insomnia, which said, "Treatment of insomnia should start with the assessment and necessary correction of sleep hygiene and habits."

Sleep specialists have embraced the term "sleep hygiene" to refer to the basic "dos and don'ts" for good sleep, well known even in ancient times, although past generations have been no better in observing them than people are today. But we have today something past generations lacked. Modern sleep laboratory technology enables scientists to determine scientifically what is sound advice and to assess the impact on sleep of matters on which there is a considerable body of folklore, such as having a bedtime snack or sleeping in a warm or cold room.

Good sleep habits can be cultivated in many ways. One tip is to get up every morning at the same time, regardless of when you go to sleep. This helps to set the body's internal clocks.

The "rules" described below are in essence guidelines. Some people pay no attention to any of them; indeed, they flagrantly do the opposite, yet sleep perfectly well. Others follow only those rules they do not regard as inconveniences. Most people, however, benefit from the structure that they offer and find that they both sleep better and feel and function better during the day as a result. You can only make an informed decision for yourself by giving them a fair trial. Here is the basic list:

•Get up about the same time every day, regardless of when you go to bed. This helps set the body's internal clocks and keep them synchronized, and it is a time you can control by setting an alarm clock. Going to bed at the same time each day is less important. Further, the events of normal daily life make a fixed bedtime impractical for most people; one sleep researcher is fond of saying, "We go to bed when we want to; we get up when we have to." For teenagers, the advice to get up at the same time on weekends as on school days may seem unrealistic; teens, and adults as well, often count on sleeping late on weekends to make up for sleep missed during the week. The call for regular times of awakening is not written in stone; sleeping an hour or two later than usual will not have a major impact on inner clocks. One way to recover lost sleep without disrupting body clocks may be to take an afternoon nap; try it and see. Some caution is advised, because occasional naps make some people cranky.

•Go to bed only when sleepy. You cannot force yourself to sleep if you are not sleepy. Going to bed at a certain time just because you "ought to" may be setting the stage for frustration. By tuning into your body's demands, you can better satisfy your sleep needs.

•Give yourself bedtime rituals. When you were younger, you probably had a favorite bedtime story, one you liked to hear over and over, night after night. As you grow older, you can still take advantage of simple routines to help you sleep. Assemble your schoolbooks and put them by the door; set out tomorrow's clothes; brush your hair; or pick any routine that you can do easily whether or not you are sleeping at home. Some people carry these to extremes: The writer

Do not try to go to bed before you are sleepy. Doing so only leads to frustration and the perception that you are having trouble falling asleep.

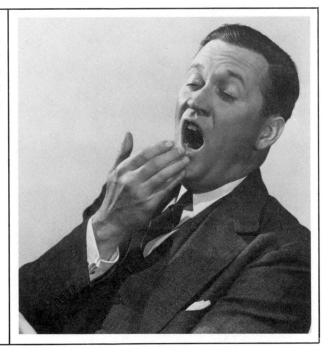

Charles Dickens insisted that the head of his bed always point north; he believed that magnetic currents traveling between the North and South poles would pass through his body and revitalize him during sleep.

•Get enough sleep. Many people pride themselves on how little sleep they get, as if they were engaging in a heroic act. The simple fact is that if you do not get enough sleep, you will feel sleepy. If you do get enough, you will feel alert and sharp and will not constantly be thinking, How am I going to get through the rest of the day? Although getting more sleep cannot guarantee that you will excel in sports or academics, it should make it more likely that you will do your best. At sleep conferences, a leading researcher frequently cites a report that he admits is unverified, but that he believes is entirely plausible. It concerns a college at which residents of an entire dormitory agreed to get an extra hour's sleep for a semester. When grades came in, their average had moved

Sleep studies show that regular, rigorous exercise is a real boon in the quest for a good night's sleep. However, avoid strenuous exertion right before bedtime, because this can rev you up.

up to a B from a C+, whereas residents of a comparable dormitory who had not altered their sleep maintained their previous C+ average.

•Do not stay in bed excessively long. This promotes a tendency to wake and doze, wake and doze, and quite understandably contributes to the perception of restless sleep. Sleep specialists say you need enough sleep to feel refreshed, but you need not try to squeeze the last drop of sleep out of every night.

•Exercise regularly, preferably in the late afternoon. Sleep laboratory studies show that both regular vigorous exercise, such as jogging or squash, in the late afternoon, and mild exercise, such as simple stretching or walking, two or three hours before bedtime, aid sleep. Vigorous exercise too close to bedtime will rev you up and make it hard to get to sleep. Vigorous exercise in the morning may help you get going for the day and may suit your schedule, but it does not seem to have any impact on nighttime sleep. A heavy workout now and then will not benefit sleep, but people who exercise regularly sleep better than those who do not.

•Avoid caffeine near bedtime. Even if you do not notice any difference in how long it takes to fall asleep, caffeine may make your sleep more restless.

•Avoid smoking at bedtime. Nicotine is a stimulant, too, and may make you awaken more often during the night.

•Avoid alcohol at bedtime. Alcohol is deceptive, in that it seems to make you sleepy. The trouble is that as it is burned by the body, it triggers frequent awakenings and often anxious dreams.

•Soundproof your bedroom. You never get used to traffic noise or airplane flyovers; they disturb sleep, even if you do not awaken completely. Noise is a key reason shift workers who must sleep during the day get less sleep and sleep more poorly than those who sleep at night. But even whispered words can take you into a lighter sleep stage. That is especially true if the word has emotional relevance for you; a prime example would be your name. If sounds are particularly bothersome, mask them with "white" noise from an air conditioner or a fan. You can also use the static of a bedside radio when tuned to the end of the FM band.

•Lightproof your bedroom, too. Yes, even if your eyes are closed, light gets through, and light has a rousing effect.

As much as possible, avoid worrying at bedtime. Set aside some specific time during the day to deal with troubling thoughts.

If sunlight streams into your room in the morning, it can awaken you before the alarm goes off.

•Adjust room temperature. There is no magic number; it seems that everyone has a personal "best" thermostat setting. Sleep lab studies have shown that when room temperatures exceed 75°F, sleep deteriorates; people awaken frequently, spend more time in lighter sleep stages, and sleep less. But when temperatures are as low as 54°F, people have more emotion-filled and anxious dreams.

•Eat with sleep in mind. A high-carbohydrate supper, such as pasta, may foster sleepiness. A light high-carbohydrate bedtime snack, such as fruit juice and cookies, may keep you from waking with hunger pangs during the night. (See also Chapter 5.)

•Reserve your bed and bedroom for sleep. If you can find any other space to do your homework, study for exams, talk on the phone, or watch television, do it. By keeping such activities out of the bedroom, you also help keep thoughts about them from interfering with your sleep. Further, if the television is in your bedroom, it may prove too tempting to watch it rather than sleep.

•Avoid worrying at bedtime. Before you say, That's impossible! note that the key is not to "avoid worrying," but to avoid doing so "at bedtime." Psychologists suggest bedtime "worriers" set aside another time — say 20 to 30 minutes after supper — to focus on whatever is bothering them. Many people find it helps to write down their problems and to list all possible solutions. If you find worried thoughts are intruding into your consciousness during the day, try telling yourself, This is not my time to worry; I'll deal with this later. Then, do it!

•Do not stay in bed fretting if you cannot sleep. After 10 or 15 minutes of wakefulness, go to another room and read or watch television until you feel sleepy. This approach is described further in Chapter 7.

•Do not take sleeping pills without first talking to your doctor. The problems associated with sleeping pills are described in Chapters 3 and 4.

•Do not lounge around and take it easy, even after a sleepless night. Keeping busy counters drowsiness. The more sleep you have missed, the more you need large body activity, like walking or other exercise, instead of small muscle activity, like reading or watching TV.

•Keep a daily sleep log if you have frequent bad nights. In the same way that recording every mouthful helps many people diet, keeping track of sleep habits often shows how they can be improved. Jot down what time you go to bed, get up, consume coffee and alcohol, exercise, and other habits you think might affect your sleep. Keep the sleep log for a week or two; it usually takes about that long for patterns to become apparent.

The man in this 19th-century lithograph is flooded with memories and cannot sleep. One insomniac said that a few restless nights can make it seem as if "this is the way you will live for the rest of your life."

CHAPTER 7

HELP FOR TROUBLED SLEEPERS

Most people can take an occasional bad night in stride. But after a few bad nights, as one insomniac relates, "You think this is the way you will live for the rest of your life." Unfortunately, the more people worry about their sleep, and the harder they try to sleep, the worse they usually end up sleeping. And the worse they sleep, the more they worry. Although stress, as noted in Chapter 2, is far from the only cause of insomnia, it probably is the number one cause of insomnia in young adults.

For insomnia that lasts three or four weeks or longer, you should see your family doctor or internist. But, assuming various illnesses have been ruled out, you will benefit from giving some thought to the types of stressful situations in which you suffer insomnia and trying to figure out ways to keep them from affecting you.

One sleep specialist suggests that chronic insomnia is more like being low on cash than having an illness. If your pockets are nearly empty, you have to count your pennies before trying to buy something and sometimes have to go without it; similarly, if you tend to be a poor sleeper, you have to stack the odds for good sleep in your favor and try not to get too upset when you do not sleep well. Following the sleep hygiene techniques outlined in the previous chapter is an important first step.

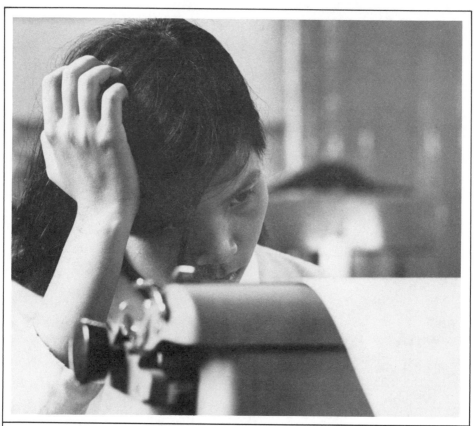

Depression is a common cause of insomnia. Frequently, successful treatment of an underlying emotional disorder can automatically relieve or eliminate altogether the sleep disturbance.

But suppose you have a quiz tomorrow, more homework than you will be able to do tonight, and you have just had a fight with your best friend. Is there anything you can do today to help yourself sleep better tonight?

Happily, the answer is yes. And it does not involve the use of sleeping pills or other drugs. If you do all you can today to alleviate these stresses — study for the test, look over even the part of the homework that you cannot finish, maybe pick up the phone and try to patch things up with your friend, or at least, devise a plan for working things out — then, when you get into bed, you can say to yourself, I've given these things my best shot.

You also can take comfort in knowing that a little lost sleep is no big deal; later in this chapter, you will find specific ways to cope with lost sleep. But now let us take a look at some of the helpful techniques that sleep specialists often advise for people prone to insomnia in times of stress.

There is essentially a supermarket full of choices here, but no single one works for everyone, and no single one appears to be appreciably more effective than any other. Only by trial and error will you find which one works best for you. Sleep specialists say that you have to stick with one or two approaches for roughly five weeks. Think of it as an activity like dieting. Usually, people who do well on a diet are those who follow a structured program. Dieting for just a few days seldom makes much difference in what you see on the bathroom scale. Moreover, the ideal diet, like the ideal way to overcome insomnia, is not a one-shot deal, but a strategy that helps you introduce meaningful changes into your daily life. A discussion of the most commonly recommended techniques for combating insomnia follows.

Sleep Restriction

Sleep restriction is a recently developed anti-insomnia technique based on the finding that many insomniacs spend excessive amounts of time in bed, hoping to make up for lost sleep. In a misguided effort to make up for lost sleep, they may start going to bed earlier and earlier, logging eight, nine, or more hours in bed. But they are miserable, because they sleep only five or six of those hours.

The strategy of sleep restriction limits sleep severely and abruptly until the sleeper is sleeping solidly for as long as he or she is in bed; then the sleep time is extended gradually, until the sleeper is getting as much sleep as desired.

Implementation of the sleep restriction technique begins by keeping track of your sleep habits for two weeks and writing down when you go to bed and awaken during the night, as well as when you get out of bed in the morning. The average amount of sleep you get becomes the maximum amount of time you should stay in bed on your new schedule.

In the beginning, you will go to bed much later than usual and stay in bed only as long as you actually sleep, even if that is only three or four hours. You should get up at the same time each morning. Do not nap during the day, even though you will probably find that you are extremely sleepy. The extra sleepiness should, however, help you to fall asleep quickly at night.

Once you can sleep at least 90% of your time in bed for 5 days in a row, you may reward yourself by going to bed 15 minutes earlier. But if you do not manage to sleep at least 90% of your time in bed for 5 days in a row, you should cut back your time in bed even more. This sounds harsh, but most people begin to sleep better within a week or two.

After a few months, you should be sleeping as long as you want. It takes a lot of determination to force yourself to stay up several hours later than usual, especially after a few days, when sleepiness can really hit you hard. And it is tough to drag yourself out of bed in the morning when you do not feel well rested. That is why the use of this technique usually is not advised on a do-it-yourself basis, but rather under the supervision of a sleep specialist experienced in its application.

Use your bedroom and bed only for sleeping if you are having restless nights. Avoid all other activities, such as doing homework or watching television, in this room.

Stimulus Control

The aim of stimulus control is to get the upper hand on those characteristics of bed and bedroom that keep you wide-eyed instead of deep in slumber. The basic rules are as follows:

- Go to bed only when you are sleepy.

- Use your bed and bedroom only for sleep.

- If you do not fall asleep in 10 to 15 minutes, get up and go to another room. It is hard to leave a warm bed. If it is cold in your home, keep a robe or a blanket to wrap around you near your bed. Read or watch television; do not lift weights or pedal an exercise bike.

- Do not snack.

- Go back to bed only when you are sleepy.

- If you do not fall asleep soon, get out of bed again.

- Set an alarm clock and get up at the same time every day. Do not sleep late on weekends — at least, no more than an hour or two.

- Do not nap during the day; tough it out until bedtime.

Cognitive (Mental) Focusing

If you cannot stand getting out of bed, even though you are wide awake, do not lie there fretting. It probably will not help to tell yourself not to worry, unless you have planned in advance to think about something else. One psychologist suggests that you pretend you are watching a special television; get rid of the bad worries channel by switching to another station.

Try one of the focusing approaches below and practice it for 30 minutes a day, so that during the night, you can easily swing into gear. Here is the "how to" list:

- Focus on your physical surroundings or on a task that interests you: Count the tiles in the floor or ceiling. Study how your desk chair is put together. Read. Watch television.
- Focus on thoughts: Recite a poem. Count backward from 100 by 7s. Mentally paint a large number on your wall using strokes from a tiny brush.

•Focus on how your body feels: Where does the sheet touch your skin? Where are you warm or cold? Where do you itch?

•Focus on imaginary scenes: Remember how great it felt to be on the beach last summer, with the sun warming your skin? Remember how cozy it was to sit by the fire with friends, everyone leaning back, relaxed, comfortable?

Monotonous Stimulation

Ocean waves that beat against the shore and then recede, wind that rustles the leaves, a heart beating steadily, and similar sounds relax most people and make it easier for them to fall asleep. For centuries, "counting sheep" has been a standard insomnia remedy, and scientists now know why. People in a sleep lab study who listened to tones that alternated with silence in two-second intervals fell asleep faster than when they listened to either total silence or a monotonous sound. The tones were even more successful in inducing sleep when people had to count them, having an effect comparable to that of counting sheep, a distracting activity that takes the mind off unwanted thoughts.

Relaxation

There are numerous methods of relaxation. Most public libraries have a good supply of books on the subject. All of the following methods are more effective with daily practice sessions repeated 2 or 3 times a day and lasting about 20 minutes. Some of the major methods are as follows:

•Progressive relaxation is a method of tensing and relaxing various muscle groups. Here, you learn to tune in to all the muscle groups in your body and gain control over feelings of tension.

•Autogenic training involves suggesting to yourself that you feel warmth and heaviness in various parts of the body. By the time you complete a full survey of the body, you should be in a calm state in which it will be easy to fall asleep.

•Meditation focuses concentration on a single phrase or sound, sometimes known as a "mantra."

Some insomniacs are wound-up psychologically or physically, but not all of them. People who are relaxed but simply

If sleep is elusive, try focusing on imaginary scenes. Picturing yourself on an ocean beach can be very relaxing.

cannot sleep actually may find it harder to rest if they pursue relaxation training, so if the techniques described in this section do not work for you, switch to another approach or consult a sleep specialist for further advice. If you cannot tell when you are tense and when you are relaxed, you may benefit from biofeedback, which can help increase awareness of various bodily states. Then it can be used to fortify relaxation skills.

Biofeedback

The biofeedback technique uses instrumentation to put you in touch with such aspects of bodily functioning as hand temperature, muscle tension, or brain wave patterns.

It is not a quick fix for insomnia. Compared to people with tension headaches, who often gain relief after 8 to 10 sessions, insomniacs may need as many as 40 sessions before improvement starts. The reason? A technique that is going to be used as you are losing consciousness needs to be over-learned, so that you can do it automatically.

You may see home biofeedback devices advertised widely in "high tech" catalogs and even general interest magazines. Sleep specialists say they may be helpful as an aid to relaxation used in conjunction with professional training, but that they are seldom effective as a do-it-yourself method. A key reason for this is that insomniacs often practice at the wrong times or for too short a period. Then they quit. It is not the devices themselves that are at fault, but the way they are used.

The Bottom Line

Sleeping pills are, at best, a temporary solution to troubled sleeping. Ideally, you will become proficient in a technique that can take the place of a pill. A bonus is that many of the approaches described above also can help ease stress in other areas of your life.

Sleep specialists say that even if you get as little as half of your usual amount of sleep, you can — by following certain rules — do everything you ordinarily do about as well as you ordinarily do it. Here are 10 tested tips:

1. *Socialize.* Interacting with other people combats sleepiness. At school, you will probably do fine if you have to answer a teacher's question or give a speech. But when you must listen to a lecture or read an assignment, beware; that is when sleepiness catches up with you.

If you go to a party after missing some sleep the night before, you probably will not suffer from your lost sleep. But leave the driving to someone else. And be even more than usually cautious about consuming alcohol; it hits you harder when you are sleepy.

2. *Try your hardest.* When you have to finish a paper by tomorrow or cram for an exam, determination helps. But because it is harder to keep going when you are both sleepy and alone, it is wiser not to tackle these activities solo. Study with a friend; quiz each other. Or write your paper in the library where the activity of other people will help keep you awake.

3. *Pay attention to your body clocks.* People are most alert during their normal waking hours, even if they have missed some sleep the night before. Most people are sharpest in the morning, sleepiest in the midafternoon. Learn to predict your own best and worst times; then act accordingly.

If you have to sacrifice some sleep to complete a big assignment or to study, is it better to stay up late or get up early? You have probably guessed that the answer depends on personal preference. Some people naturally gravitate to the night hours, whereas others are early birds. It is, however, easier to stay up later, because body clocks readjust more naturally to later hours. If you do get up early, try to get to bed earlier the next night. If you stay up late, you will probably find it harder to fall asleep at your regular time, even though you may be sleepy; if you continue to stay up later, you may trick your body into thinking you have traveled into a new time zone. One way to counter this effect is to get up at the same time every morning.

There are many things you can do to counteract the effects of a poor night's sleep. Socializing with friends is one way to combat daytime sleepiness and also to relieve anxiety that can lead to insomnia.

Exercise is another way to overcome daytime drowsiness. It recharges the body physically and makes you interact with your environment, which is psychologically invigorating.

4. *Exercise*. Physical activity counters sleepiness because it makes you interact with your environment.

5. *Light up your life*. Going outside for at least a few minutes as soon as possible after awakening — before you have had breakfast or showered — seems to help people become more alert faster. Most people know this intuitively; that is why they throw open the curtains or raise the shades first thing in the morning.

6. *Take a nap*. Do it at midday, when you are naturally sleepiest. Do not nap for more than 90 minutes or you might sabotage your nighttime sleep. If you are going to get less sleep than usual at night, take as long a nap as is possible without interruption; do not divide daytime sleep into "sleep breaks." The longer you can nap solidly, the more rested you are likely to feel.

7. *Eat lightly*. Choose energy-giving proteins. Avoid sleep-inducing carbohydrates.

8. *Get a lift from caffeine*. Stopping for coffee or a soda often involves company, so you get the added stimulation of interaction with other people.

9. *Go to bed early.* You do not have to compensate fully for sleep missed, but if you are trying to beat a sleep loss, you can put an extra hour or two of sleep to good use. Even if you do not fall asleep right away, getting to bed early by itself is restorative.

10. *See your doctor if daytime sleepiness persists.* If you are so sleepy that you cannot concentrate during the day, or if you keep falling asleep when you do not intend to, arrange a physical examination. Other than simply not getting enough sleep, the most common cause of persistent daytime sleepiness in adolescents is a disorder called narcolepsy. (See Chapter 4.) Mononucleosis is another disorder that causes daytime sleepiness, and sometimes the sleepiness continues after the illness seems to have run its course.

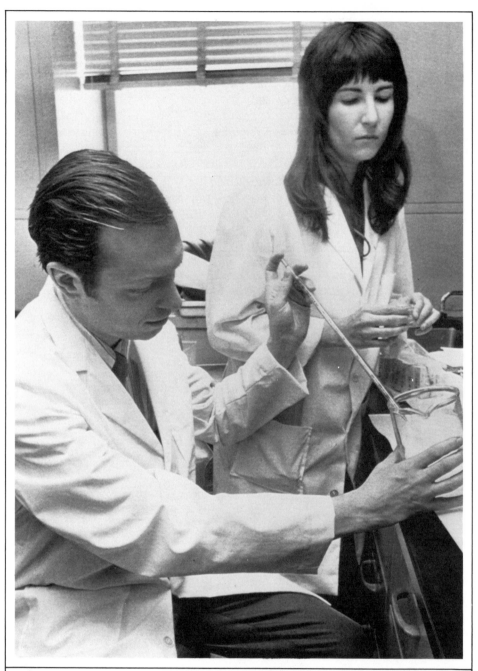

The research of Drs. Solomon Snyder and Candace Pert uncovered substances, called endorphins, that the body produces naturally to fight pain. Similar studies may lead to the discoveries of body chemicals that promote relaxation and sleep.

CHAPTER 8

NEW DIRECTIONS IN RESEARCH

Although scientists have demonstrated that sleep is an active process, not simply a state of semiconsciousness to which we passively succumb, the chemical "switch" that naturally occurs within our bodies to turn sleep on — and off — continues to elude researchers.

One of the most active areas of current research focuses on benzodiazepine receptors — the specific sites on nerve cell membranes in the brain to which the benzodiazepines, the drugs most commonly used as sleeping pills, must attach in order to do their work.

It was only in 1973 that Solomon Snyder and Candace Pert at the Johns Hopkins University School of Medicine in Baltimore found opiate receptors in the brain, the sites of action not only for painkilling drugs such as morphine and heroin, but also for pain-relieving substances the body itself manufactures, often called "endogenous opiates" (meaning "the opiates within").

The discovery of benzodiazepine receptors in 1977 by a team of Swiss and Danish researchers generated considerable excitement in scientific circles. Researchers postulated that, just as the identification of opiate receptors had led to the discovery of substances the body produces to deaden pain, so the identification of benzodiazepine receptors might

An artistic depiction of Night. Ongoing research into brain chemistry may eventually lead to the development of a "natural" sleeping pill that will make "lights out" a time of sweet repose for all.

lead to the discovery of substances the body produces to induce sleep. And in turn, it was hoped that just as the discovery of endogenous opiates is fueling the development of more effective painkilling drugs, so might the discovery of endogenous sleep inducers lead to better sleeping pills.

Although studies of neurotransmitter receptors in the brain have indeed enlarged the understanding of how neurotransmitters work, served to identify new neurotransmitters, provided new tools for figuring out how drugs work, and assisted in the development of new drugs, the search for endogenous benzodiazepines continues as of this writing.

It has, however, had some payoffs. Scientists have concocted several substances known as benzodiazepine antagonists that fit the benzodiazepine receptor, as a key fits a lock, yet have no apparent biological effect. The practical advantage is that by inserting these chemical keys into the lock, scientists can keep other keys out. Thus, such substances may be able to keep benzodiazepines from acting; theoretically, for example, they could counteract the effect of an overdose of sleeping pills or even stop the action of a sleeping pill after the user awakens in the morning, thus preventing daytime drowsiness. Further, they could even block endogenous sleep-inducing chemicals and make people more alert.

Another avenue of research into naturally occurring sleep-inducing substances has been under way for two decades at Harvard University, where scientists have extracted a substance first from brain fluid and, more recently, from the urine of sleep-deprived — and therefore, sleepy — animals. When infused into the brain of control animals, this substance, which the researchers call "Factor S" (the S stands for sleep), makes the animals sleep longer. How it works remains to be clarified.

Scientists hope that finding the chemical switch that turns sleep on will lead to the development of a more "natural" sleeping pill, one that is more effective, more likely to produce normal sleep, and less likely to have unwanted side effects than currently available medications. Learning how sleep turns on may also lead to finding ways to turn it off; that is, to discovering ways to counteract sleepiness and foster alertness.

Future drugs, then, may enable more of us to achieve the state of happy equilibrium that Shakespeare may have had in mind when he paid this tribute to sleep in his classic tragedy *Macbeth*:

Sleep that knits up the ravell'd sleave of care,
The death of each day's life, sore labour's bath,
Balm of hurt minds, great nature's second course,
Chief nourisher in life's feast.

APPENDIX I

FOR MORE INFORMATION

Some 100 disorders of sleeping and waking harm personal health and quality of life and endanger public safety by contributing to traffic and industrial accidents. These disorders include problems in falling or staying asleep, staying awake, and adhering to a consistent sleep/wake schedule, along with sleepwalking, bedwetting, nightmares, and other problems that interfere with sleep.

Sleep disorders are diagnosed and treated by specialists in neurology, pulmonary medicine, psychiatry, psychology, pediatrics, and other fields. The Association of Professional Sleep Societies, founded to increase awareness of sleep disorders among the public and professionals, is the field's major national organization. It represents 2,500 clinicians and researchers with training and proven competence in sleep disorder medicine.

For more information about specific sleep disorders and names of sleep disorder centers near you, contact the association at the following address:

The Association of Professional Sleep Societies
604 Second St. SW
Rochester, MN 55902

APPENDIX II

SLEEP/WAKE DIARY

Use the three-day sample below as a guide to prepare your sleep/wake diary. You will need to keep a diary for at least a week to get a good sense of your sleep patterns. Record all times in hours and minutes, e.g., "6:15." Mark all sleep periods, including naps, with a dark line. Note events or activities that seem to harm or help you sleep, e.g., coffee, alcohol, stressful day, day off from work, argument with parents or spouse, trip, and, for women, time of menstrual cycle.

Use the following abbreviations:
- **M:** meals
- **S:** snacks
- **P:** sleeping pills
- **D:** other drugs (number and list separately)
- **X:** exercise
- **A:** alarm clock

	P.M.		MIDNIGHT				A.M.			NOON			P.M.
	6	8	10	12	2	4	6	8	10	12	2	4	6
CLOCK TIME INTO BED													
CLOCK TIME TRY TO SLEEP													
MINUTES BEFORE SLEEP													
SLEEP PERIOD GRAPH			THURSDAY										
CLOCK TIME FINAL WAKE													
CLOCK TIME OUT OF BED													

CLOCK TIME INTO BED													
CLOCK TIME TRY TO SLEEP													
MINUTES BEFORE SLEEP													
SLEEP PERIOD GRAPH				FRIDAY SATURDAY									
CLOCK TIME FINAL WAKE													
CLOCK TIME OUT OF BED													

CLOCK TIME INTO BED													
CLOCK TIME TRY TO SLEEP													
MINUTES BEFORE SLEEP													
SLEEP PERIOD GRAPH			SUNDAY										
CLOCK TIME FINAL WAKE													
CLOCK TIME OUT OF BED													

Source: The American Medical Association Guide to Better Sleep, Random House, 1984.

APPENDIX III

SLEEPINESS/ALERTNESS CHART

INSTRUCTIONS

- Complete this chart during the time that you are keeping the diary.
- Select two typical CONSECUTIVE working or school days.
- Write in the days and dates you selected at the top of each chart.
- Throughout your waking hours on these days RATE yourself every two hours according to the scale to the right.
- CIRCLE the number indicating your level of alertness or sleepiness for each two-hour time period.
- CIRCLE X for those times when you were asleep.

SCALE

1. Alert. Wide Awake. Energetic.
2. Functioning at a high level, but not at peak. Able to concentrate.
3. Awake, but not fully alert.
4. A little foggy, let down.
5. Foggy. Beginning to lose interest in remaining awake. Slowed down.
6. Sleepy. Prefer to be lying down. Woozy.
7. Cannot stay awake. Sleep onset soon.
X. Asleep.

DAY ONE

Day _____ Date _____

DAY TWO

Day _____ Date _____

MID-NIGHT	A.M. PERIOD 2 4 6 8 10	NOON	P.M. PERIOD 2 4 6 8 10	MID-NIGHT	A.M. PERIOD 2 4 6 8 10	NOON	P.M. PERIOD 2 4 6 8 10	MID-NIGHT
1	1 1 1 1 1	1	1 1 1 1 1	1	1 1 1 1 1	1	1 1 1 1 1	1
2	2 2 2 2 2	2	2 2 2 2 2	2	2 2 2 2 2	2	2 2 2 2 2	2
3	3 3 3 3 3	3	3 3 3 3 3	3	3 3 3 3 3	3	3 3 3 3 3	3
4	4 4 4 4 4	4	4 4 4 4 4	4	4 4 4 4 4	4	4 4 4 4 4	4
5	5 5 5 5 5	5	5 5 5 5 5	5	5 5 5 5 5	5	5 5 5 5 5	5
6	6 6 6 6 6	6	6 6 6 6 6	6	6 6 6 6 6	6	6 6 6 6 6	6
7	7 7 7 7 7	7	7 7 7 7 7	7	7 7 7 7 7	7	7 7 7 7 7	7
X	X X X X X	X	X X X X X	X	X X X X X	X	X X X X X	X

Source: The American Medical Association Guide to Better Sleep, Random House, 1984.

APPENDIX IV

State Agencies
for the Prevention and Treatment
of Drug Abuse

ALABAMA
Department of Mental Health
Division of Mental Illness and
  Substance Abuse Community
  Programs
200 Interstate Park Drive
P.O. Box 3710
Montgomery, AL 36193
(205) 271-9253

ALASKA
Department of Health and Social
  Services
Office of Alcoholism and Drug
  Abuse
Pouch H-05-F
Juneau, AK 99811
(907) 586-6201

ARIZONA
Department of Health Services
Division of Behavioral Health
  Services
Bureau of Community Services
Alcohol Abuse and Alcoholism
  Section
2500 East Van Buren
Phoenix, AZ 85008
(602) 255-1238

Department of Health Services
Division of Behavioral Health
  Services
Bureau of Community Services
Drug Abuse Section
2500 East Van Buren
Phoenix, AZ 85008
(602) 255-1240

ARKANSAS
Department of Human Services
Office of Alcohol and Drug Abuse
  Prevention
1515 West 7th Avenue
Suite 310
Little Rock, AR 72202
(501) 371-2603

CALIFORNIA
Department of Alcohol and Drug
  Abuse
111 Capitol Mall
Sacramento, CA 95814
(916) 445-1940

COLORADO
Department of Health
Alcohol and Drug Abuse Division
4210 East 11th Avenue
Denver, CO 80220
(303) 320-6137

CONNECTICUT
Alcohol and Drug Abuse
  Commission
999 Asylum Avenue
3rd Floor
Hartford, CT 06105
(203) 566-4145

DELAWARE
Division of Mental Health
Bureau of Alcoholism and Drug
  Abuse
1901 North Dupont Highway
Newcastle, DE 19720
(302) 421-6101

DISTRICT OF COLUMBIA
Department of Human Services
Office of Health Planning and
  Development
601 Indiana Avenue, NW
Suite 500
Washington, D.C. 20004
(202) 724-5641

FLORIDA
Department of Health and
  Rehabilitative Services
Alcoholic Rehabilitation Program
1317 Winewood Boulevard
Room 187A
Tallahassee, FL 32301
(904) 488-0396

Department of Health and
  Rehabilitative Services
Drug Abuse Program
1317 Winewood Boulevard
Building 6, Room 155
Tallahassee, FL 32301
(904) 488-0900

GEORGIA
Department of Human Resources
Division of Mental Health and
  Mental Retardation
Alcohol and Drug Section
618 Ponce De Leon Avenue, NE
Atlanta, GA 30365-2101
(404) 894-4785

HAWAII
Department of Health
Mental Health Division
Alcohol and Drug Abuse Branch
1250 Punch Bowl Street
P.O. Box 3378
Honolulu, HI 96801
(808) 548-4280

IDAHO
Department of Health and Welfare
Bureau of Preventive Medicine
Substance Abuse Section
450 West State
Boise, ID 83720
(208) 334-4368

ILLINOIS
Department of Mental Health and
  Developmental Disabilities
Division of Alcoholism
160 North La Salle Street
Room 1500
Chicago, IL 60601
(312) 793-2907

Illinois Dangerous Drugs
  Commission
300 North State Street
Suite 1500
Chicago, IL 60610
(312) 822-9860

INDIANA
Department of Mental Health
Division of Addiction Services
429 North Pennsylvania Street
Indianapolis, IN 46204
(317) 232-7816

IOWA
Department of Substance Abuse
505 5th Avenue
Insurance Exchange Building
Suite 202
Des Moines, IA 50319
(515) 281-3641

KANSAS
Department of Social Rehabilitation
Alcohol and Drug Abuse Services
2700 West 6th Street
Biddle Building
Topeka, KS 66606
(913) 296-3925

KENTUCKY
Cabinet for Human Resources
Department of Health Services
Substance Abuse Branch
275 East Main Street
Frankfort, KY 40601
(502) 564-2880

LOUISIANA
Department of Health and Human
  Resources
Office of Mental Health and
  Substance Abuse
655 North 5th Street
P.O. Box 4049
Baton Rouge, LA 70821
(504) 342-2565

MAINE
Department of Human Services
Office of Alcoholism and Drug
  Abuse Prevention
Bureau of Rehabilitation
32 Winthrop Street
Augusta, ME 04330
(207) 289-2781

MARYLAND
Alcoholism Control Administration
201 West Preston Street
Fourth Floor
Baltimore, MD 21201
(301) 383-2977

State Health Department
Drug Abuse Administration
201 West Preston Street
Baltimore, MD 21201
(301) 383-3312

MASSACHUSETTS
Department of Public Health
Division of Alcoholism
755 Boylston Street
Sixth Floor
Boston, MA 02116
(617) 727-1960

Department of Public Health
Division of Drug Rehabilitation
600 Washington Street
Boston, MA 02114
(617) 727-8617

MICHIGAN
Department of Public Health
Office of Substance Abuse Services
3500 North Logan Street
P.O. Box 30035
Lansing, MI 48909
(517) 373-8603

MINNESOTA
Department of Public Welfare
Chemical Dependency Program
  Division
Centennial Building
658 Cedar Street
4th Floor
Saint Paul, MN 55155
(612) 296-4614

MISSISSIPPI
Department of Mental Health
Division of Alcohol and Drug Abuse
1102 Robert E. Lee Building
Jackson, MS 39201
(601) 359-1297

MISSOURI
Department of Mental Health
Division of Alcoholism and Drug
  Abuse
2002 Missouri Boulevard
P.O. Box 687
Jefferson City, MO 65102
(314) 751-4942

MONTANA
Department of Institutions
Alcohol and Drug Abuse Division
1539 11th Avenue
Helena, MT 59620
(406) 449-2827

NEBRASKA
Department of Public Institutions
Division of Alcoholism and Drug
Abuse
801 West Van Dorn Street
P.O. Box 94728
Lincoln, NB 68509
(402) 471-2851, Ext. 415

NEVADA
Department of Human Resources
Bureau of Alcohol and Drug Abuse
505 East King Street
Carson City, NV 89710
(702) 885-4790

NEW HAMPSHIRE
Department of Health and Welfare
Office of Alcohol and Drug Abuse
  Prevention
Hazen Drive
Health and Welfare Building
Concord, NH 03301
(603) 271-4627

NEW JERSEY
Department of Health
Division of Alcoholism
129 East Hanover Street CN 362
Trenton, NJ 08625
(609) 292-8949

Department of Health
Division of Narcotic and Drug
  Abuse Control
129 East Hanover Street CN 362
Trenton, NJ 08625
(609) 292-8949

NEW MEXICO
Health and Environment Department
Behavioral Services Division
Substance Abuse Bureau
725 Saint Michaels Drive
P.O. Box 968
Santa Fe, NM 87503
(505) 984-0020, Ext. 304

NEW YORK
Division of Alcoholism and Alcohol
  Abuse
194 Washington Avenue
Albany, NY 12210
(518) 474-5417

Division of Substance Abuse
  Services
Executive Park South
Box 8200
Albany, NY 12203
(518) 457-7629

NORTH CAROLINA
Department of Human Resources
Division of Mental Health, Mental
  Retardation and Substance Abuse
  Services
Alcohol and Drug Abuse Services
325 North Salisbury Street
Albemarle Building
Raleigh, NC 27611
(919) 733-4670

NORTH DAKOTA
Department of Human Services
Division of Alcoholism and Drug
  Abuse
State Capitol Building
Bismarck, ND 58505
(701) 224-2767

OHIO
Department of Health
Division of Alcoholism
246 North High Street
P.O. Box 118
Columbus, OH 43216
(614) 466-3543

Department of Mental Health
Bureau of Drug Abuse
65 South Front Street
Columbus, OH 43215
(614) 466-9023

OKLAHOMA
Department of Mental Health
Alcohol and Drug Programs
4545 North Lincoln Boulevard
Suite 100 East Terrace
P.O. Box 53277
Oklahoma City, OK 73152
(405) 521-0044

OREGON
Department of Human Resources
Mental Health Division
Office of Programs for Alcohol and
    Drug Problems
2575 Bittern Street, NE
Salem, OR 97310
(503) 378-2163

PENNSYLVANIA
Department of Health
Office of Drug and Alcohol
    Programs
Commonwealth and Forster Avenues
Health and Welfare Building
P.O. Box 90
Harrisburg, PA 17108
(717) 787-9857

RHODE ISLAND
Department of Mental Health,
    Mental Retardation and Hospitals
Division of Substance Abuse
Substance Abuse Administration
    Building
Cranston, RI 02920
(401) 464-2091

SOUTH CAROLINA
Commission on Alcohol and Drug
    Abuse
3700 Forest Drive
Columbia, SC 29204
(803) 758-2521

SOUTH DAKOTA
Department of Health
Division of Alcohol and Drug Abuse
523 East Capitol, Joe Foss Building
Pierre, SD 57501
(605) 773-4806

TENNESSEE
Department of Mental Health and
    Mental Retardation
Alcohol and Drug Abuse Services
505 Deaderick Street
James K. Polk Building,
    Fourth Floor
Nashville, TN 37219
(615) 741-1921

TEXAS
Commission on Alcoholism
809 Sam Houston State Office
    Building
Austin, TX 78701
(512) 475-2577
Department of Community Affairs
Drug Abuse Prevention Division
2015 South Interstate Highway 35
P.O. Box 13166
Austin, TX 78711
(512) 443-4100

UTAH
Department of Social Services
Division of Alcoholism and Drugs
150 West North Temple
Suite 350
P.O. Box 2500
Salt Lake City, UT 84110
(801) 533-6532

VERMONT
Agency of Human Services
Department of Social and
    Rehabilitation Services
Alcohol and Drug Abuse Division
103 South Main Street
Waterbury, VT 05676
(802) 241-2170

VIRGINIA
Department of Mental Health and
Mental Retardation
Division of Substance Abuse
109 Governor Street
P.O. Box 1797
Richmond, VA 23214
(804) 786-5313

WASHINGTON
Department of Social and Health
Service
Bureau of Alcohol and Substance
Abuse
Office Building—44 W
Olympia, WA 98504
(206) 753-5866

WEST VIRGINIA
Department of Health
Office of Behavioral Health Services
Division on Alcoholism and Drug
Abuse
1800 Washington Street East
Building 3 Room 451
Charleston, WV 25305
(304) 348-2276

WISCONSIN
Department of Health and Social
Services
Division of Community Services
Bureau of Community Programs
Alcohol and Other Drug Abuse
Program Office
1 West Wilson Street
P.O. Box 7851
Madison, WI 53707
(608) 266-2717

WYOMING
Alcohol and Drug Abuse Programs
Hathaway Building
Cheyenne, WY 82002
(307) 777-7115, Ext. 7118

GUAM
Mental Health & Substance Abuse
Agency
P.O. Box 20999
Guam 96921

PUERTO RICO
Department of Addiction Control
Services
Alcohol Abuse Programs
P.O. Box B-Y Rio Piedras Station
Rio Piedras, PR 00928
(809) 763-5014

Department of Addiction Control
Services
Drug Abuse Programs
P.O. Box B-Y Rio Piedras Station
Rio Piedras, PR 00928
(809) 764-8140

VIRGIN ISLANDS
Division of Mental Health,
Alcoholism & Drug Dependency
Services
P.O. Box 7329
Saint Thomas, Virgin Islands 00801
(809) 774-7265

AMERICAN SAMOA
LBJ Tropical Medical Center
Department of Mental Health Clinic
Pago Pago, American Samoa 96799

TRUST TERRITORIES
Director of Health Services
Office of the High Commissioner
Saipan, Trust Territories 96950

Further Reading

Borbely, Alexander. *Secrets of Sleep*. New York: Basic Books, 1986.

Dryer, Bernard and Ellen S. Kaplan. *Inside Insomnia*. New York: Villard Books, 1986.

Hales, Diane. *The Complete Book of Sleep*. Reading, MA: Addison-Wesley, 1981.

Hartmann, Ernest. *The Sleeping Pill*. New Haven, CT: University Press, 1978.

Hauri, Peter. *The Sleep Disorders*. Kalamazoo, MI: The Upjohn Company, 1982.

Lamberg, Lynne. *The American Medical Association Guide to Better Sleep*. New York: Random House, 1984.

Lambley, Peter. *Insomnia and Other Sleeping Problems*. New York: Pinnacle Books, 1982.

Maxmen, Jerrold S. *A Good Night's Sleep*. New York: W. W. Norton and Co., 1981.

Mendelson, Wallace B. *The Use and Misuse of Sleeping Pills*. New York: Plenum Medical Book Company, 1980.

Phillips, Elliott Richard. *Get a Good Night's Sleep*. Englewood Cliffs, NJ: Prentice-Hall, 1983.

Wurtman, Judith J. *Managing Your Mind and Mood Through Food*. New York: Rawson Associates, 1986.

Glossary

addiction a condition caused by repeated drug use characterized by a compulsive urge to continue using the drug, a tendency to increase the dosage, and physiological and/or psychological dependence

amino acid any one of a number of organic compounds containing an amino group and a carboxyl; the fundamental building blocks of proteins

barbiturates drugs that have a depressant effect on the central nervous system and respiration. They have toxic side effects and, when used excessively, can lead to tolerance, dependence, and even death

benzodiazepines minor tranquilizers thought to enhance the effects of the neurotransmitter GABA. Some examples are flurazepam (Dalmane) and diazepam (Valium)

caffeine a central nervous system stimulant found in coffee, tea, cocoa, various soft drinks, and often in combination with other drugs to enhance their effects

chloral hydrate transparent crystals used to induce sleep, producing sleep patterns close to normal

dopamine a catecholamine active in the synthesis of norepinephrine; also acts as a neurotransmitter in the brain

GABA gamma-aminobutyric acid; the brain's major inhibitory neurotransmitter which reduces the activity of the nerve cells it comes in contact with

half-life the amount of time required by the body to inactivate half of the drug taken

insomnia inability to sleep, or sleep interrupted or ended by periods of wakefulness. Can be chronic or short-term

melatonin a hormone produced by the pineal gland. Has possible sleep-inducing properties

narcolepsy a chronic illness characterized by recurring attacks of drowsiness and sleep which the patient is unable to control

neurotransmitter a chemical released by neurons that transmits nerve impulses across a synapse

nicotine a stimulant found in tobacco that causes dependence in habitual smokers

norepinephrine a neurotransmitter found in the autonomic nervous system

NREM "quiet sleep" characterized by slow brain activity, low blood pressure, and restlessness of the arms and legs

opiates compounds from the milky juice of the poppy plant *Papaver somniferum* including opium, morphine, codeine, and their derivatives (such as heroin)

physical dependence adaption of the body to the presence of a drug such that its absence produces withdrawal symptoms

psychological dependence a condition in which the drug user craves a drug to maintain a sense of well-being and feels discomfort when deprived of it

receptor a specialized component of a cell that combines with a chemical substance to alter the function of a cell; for example nerve-cell receptors combine with neurotransmitters

REM "active sleep" characterized by vivid dreams, rapid eye movement, irregular brain activity, and paralysis of the arms and legs

sedative a drug that produces calmness, relaxation, and sleep

serotonin a compound thought to act as a neurotransmitter in affecting sleep functions; widely distributed throughout the body, it acts similarly to the histamines in combating inflammation

stimulant any drug that increases brain activity and produces the sensation of greater energy, euphoria, and increased alertness

tolerance a decrease of susceptibility to the effects of a drug due to its continued administration resulting in the user's need to increase the drug dosage to achieve the effects previously experienced

tranquilizer an antianxiety drug that has calming and relaxing effects; Librium and Valium are tranquilizers

tryptophan an amino acid employed by the body in making serotonin

tyrosine an amino acid used by the body in producing catecholamines

withdrawal the physiological and psychological effects of discontinued use of a drug

PICTURE CREDITS

Index

Lynne Lamberg is a free-lance medical journalist and editor who lives in Baltimore, Maryland. She is the author of *The American Medical Association Guide to Better Sleep.* Her work in the scientific field has appeared in *The Journal of the American Medical Association, American Medical News,* and *The Medical Tribune.*

Solomon H. Snyder, M.D. is Distinguished Service Professor of Neuroscience, Pharmacology and Psychiatry at The Johns Hopkins University School of Medicine. He has served as president of the Society for Neuroscience and in 1978 received the Albert Lasker Award in Medical Research. He has authored *Uses of Marijuana, Madness and the Brain, The Troubled Mind, Biological Aspects of Mental Disorder,* and edited *Perspective in Neuropharmacology: A Tribute to Julius Axelrod.* Professor Snyder was a research associate with Dr. Axelrod at the National Institutes of Health.

Barry L. Jacobs, Ph.D., is currently a professor in the program of neuroscience at Princeton University. Professor Jacobs is author of *Serotonin Neurotransmission and Behavior* and *Hallucinogens: Neurochemical, Behavioral and Clinical Perspectives.* He has written many journal articles in the field of neuroscience and contributed numerous chapters to books on behavior and brain science. He has been a member of several panels of the National Institute of Mental Health.

Joann Ellison Rodgers, M.S. (Columbia), became Deputy Director of Public Affairs and Director of Media Relations for the Johns Hopkins Medical Institutions in Baltimore, Maryland, in 1984 after 18 years as an award-winning science journalist and widely read columnist for the Hearst newspapers.